SHORT
CUTS
TO GREAT
GARDENS

SHORT
CUTS
TO GREAT
GARDENS

NIGEL COLBORN

conran
OCTOPUS

First published in Great Britain in 1993
by Conran Octopus Limited
a part of Octopus Publishing Group
2-4 Heron Quays
London E14 4JP

www.conran-octopus.co.uk

This paperback edition published in 1999,
reprinted in 2000

10 9 8 7 6 5 4 3 2

British Library Cataloguing-in-Publication Data.
A catalogue record for this book is available
from the British Library.

ISBN 1 85029 779 7

Project Editor Sarah Pearce

Editor Jackie Matthews

Art Editor Prue Bucknall

Picture Research Jessica Walton

Production Julia Golding

Illustrators Gill Tomblin, Vanessa Luff

Typeset by Servis Filmsetting Limited,
Manchester

Printed in China

CONTENTS

INTRODUCTION

How delightful to take a summer stroll, unhurried and relaxed, through an historic garden! Think of the venerable lawns in an old college quadrangle, the ancient trees in some of the world's botanic gardens or the stately parterres of a palace landscape.

Such gardens seem timeless and one wonders what their creators would think of them now, were they to come back and walk among the twentieth century sightseers and plant enthusiasts. One wonders how they had the patience to work for such a long-term result – a result which they knew they would not live to see?

On a much smaller scale, it is just as enjoyable to unwind and relax in a well-established private garden. Large trees, tall hedges, carefully planted, colour-co-ordinated borders, naturalistic rock gardens, terraces, raised beds, water features and the wild garden all contribute to a feeling of maturity and of permanence.

You might think that such pleasing results are only achievable with horticultural skill and a liberal measure of artistic flair, but, amazingly, these qualities are within easy reach of any gardener. Even beginners can soon develop the knack of clever growing and judicious planting, gradually building up to more challenging plants and more complicated projects as their craft develops and their confidence grows.

The only thing a gardener cannot find in a seed packet or at the garden centre is time. Plants may take several seasons to establish themselves, some trees grow slowly and will not flower for a decade, walls and paving, although quickly installed, take several summer bakes and winter freezes to mellow. For a garden to mature to that special elegance where hard edges are softened by vegetation, where brick and stonework has collected a natural garnish of moss and lichen and where flowering plants have created their own self-perpetuating colonies, you need patience. But, although you cannot buy time, there are plenty of ways in which you can reduce the lead time to maturity.

The purpose of this book is to show ways of minimizing the wait. Whether the site is on virgin territory or is an old property suffering from years of neglect, the following pages show you how to make your garden look good quickly and then go on getting better and better. Even on a tight schedule – and a tight budget – you will be able to create a garden of good standing with a long future.

With thoughtful planning, skilful design, judicious planting and a sizeable injection of low cunning, anyone can take the short-cut route to creating an illusion of maturity within their plot and thus create a truly great garden in the minimum of time.

1

CREATING THE DREAM GARDEN

Gardens mean so many things to so many people, so what, precisely, is a good garden? To a keen plantsman, it is the repository for a precious collection. He or she may not be too bothered about how well designed it is as long as the plants are happy and healthy. To someone with artistic sensibilities, on the other hand, design and layout are all important. But, since so many gardeners combine a love of plants with aesthetic taste, the best gardens accommodate a wide and interesting assortment of plants within a pleasing and original design.

Fortunately, the short-cut garden is no exception to this, since arriving at early maturity does not necessarily lead to a dropping of standards, just a different way of achieving objectives. Your first step, however, is deciding just what you want and how much time you are willing to devote to it, either in setting it up or maintaining it once it is established.

Established though this garden may look, much of the display comes from perennials and roses flowering on a single season's growth.

A GOOD GARDEN

A good garden needs to provide more than just a visual feast. The demands put upon it vary according to the needs of its owner.

A social area with furniture and, if possible, a quiet arbour or seat where solitude can be enjoyed are generally necessary. For young families, a play area is essential. That means plenty of lawn space, a sand pit, a place for outdoor toys and swings or climbing frames. Such objects might be seen to clash with your aesthetic needs, but in a well-designed and planted garden, they will not.

In these days of threatened environments, gardens are becoming increasingly important as wildlife refuges and for many people wildlife has become a key feature of the well-planned garden. Uninvited guests, particularly biting insects or reptiles, may not be to everyone's taste, but who could dislike the presence of songbirds or butterflies?

In earlier centuries, great ornamental gar-dens were laid out to impress, announcing their owners' wealth and power. Modern private gardens are far more intimate, of course, but they can still be a means of impressing visitors, and front gardens, where they are visible to passers-by, are usually planted quite differently from the more personal environs at the back.

Wanting to impress visitors is not simply vanity. If you are trying to sell your house, for instance, potential buyers will react much more favourably to an impressive garden than to an immature planting or to a neglected mess. In this case, your need for a mature-looking garden may be urgent.

Home-grown food is again becoming popular and people are increasingly setting aside some of their land to grow at least a proportion of their own food. Interestingly, a well-designed, well-stocked kitchen garden can look as beautiful as the smartest flower border and, because it reaches maturity in a single season (pages 20–21), makes a pretty good short-cut device as well.

ABIDING INTEREST

No matter what use it is put to, a good garden has a timeless quality. From day to day, as the seasons advance, it changes its appearance. There are periods, usually in early summer, when everything looks superb and other times when the planting is more low key. But there should never be a waning of interest; the garden should be as enticing in winter as in summer, even though it then has considerably less colour. In cold climates, where frost is a constant feature throughout the winter period, trees and shrubs are the only plants likely to contribute anything significant.

▶ **Plant evergreens to harmonize with the stark, winter outlines of deciduous trees. From glossy leaved hollies to all the differently shaped conifers in their wide-ranging hues of gold, green and blue-green, they offer hundreds of ways of enriching the winter garden's flora.**

DESIGN

Part of the technique of making effective short cuts is careful planning, so knowing exactly how you want the garden laid out is an important first step, to be taken well before the first plant goes in!

▶ **Allow for social areas – patios, terraces or even a plunge or swimming pool. These will need paving, preferably with materials that look old for a lived-in look.**

▶ **If you are constructing a new wall, think about installing fixtures to carry climbers and encourage plant cover to develop at maximum speed. Vine eyes and wires or other supports can often be built in as the walls are erected.**

▶ **Plan arrangements of beds and borders to accommodate both immature and large plants as well as very dense plantings.**

PLANTING PRINCIPLES

The principles of planting and plant association apply as much to the short-cut garden as to any other. The idea of the short cut is simply to achieve those principles as quickly as possible.

Planting must be for shape as well as for colour, texture and that indefinable quality of certain plants loosely termed 'character'. The plants to use fall into three main categories.

Every garden needs its profile. Some of the outline will already have been provided by buildings, structures, large trees outside the boundary, pergolas and so on. The remainder is provided by planting. Outline plants, usually trees and shrubs which come in a series of shapes from tall and thin to low and spreading, are the ones that show up most in winter when there are fewer colourful flowers about.

Below the outline comes the understorey. These are the plants that occur naturally below trees and can be seen on woodland floors, along roadsides, at the margins of fields or in hay meadows. In gardens they consist of herbaceous plants and small shrubs.

Among the background planting, you need something bigger or bolder – plants which draw attention to themselves, plants which grow dramatically large in a short span of time or

ABOVE *An instant garden effect is quickly achievable with paving and containers which hold large, mature plants. Argyranthemum, ivies and clipped box provide a solid background to the planting while shorter-lived day lilies and osteospermums come and go as the seasons progress.*

OPPOSITE *Quick-growing annuals in containers and speedy perennials work hard to give an effect while slower shrubs and climbers develop. Introducing plant material softens the rawness of newly built structures.*

ABOVE *In addition to providing a valuable winter outline, pine, birches and shrubs make a tall backdrop for herbaceous plants selected to create a golden theme. Even while relatively young, trees and shrubs create a solid outline for the rest of the planting.*

RIGHT *Dahlias, delphiniums and golden rod blend well with gaillardias and a selection of hardy annuals in a late summer border. A colourful climax is achievable in a single season when vigorous herbaceous plants are used.*

shrubs that are suddenly smothered with bright flowers. I dub these 'star performers' because they make a bold, often very loud statement, when they are at their best, but are only in evidence for a short part of the gardening year. But they must never detract from the overall planting harmony. A sharp contrast can be as effective as a crash of cymbals at the right point in a piece of music, but a horrendous colour clash could be likened to the percussionist dropping a cymbal at the wrong moment.

▶ **Trees and shrubs are generally the most useful outline plants, as they come in lots of different shapes and sizes, from tall and thin to low and spreading. Trees contribute spreading winter branches and summer shade. Evergreens become prominent in winter, too, fading into the background in summer when the rapidly growing herbaceous plants take centre stage.**

▶ **Group colours, textures and characters in pleasing associations so that there are changes in mood, not only from one part of the garden to another, but also throughout the four seasons.**

▶ **Dot star performers among background planting to provide changing points of interest. Rhododendrons, lilies between shrubs, giant mulleins, a sudden burst of tulips in a mixed border can all make a conspicuous contribution.**

SHORT CUTS

The main thrust of this book is to show how it is possible, with special planting and design strategies, to simulate maturity and stature in a garden in a relatively short time. By maturity I mean something to be measured by appearances, rather than by chronology.

The idea of using special tricks to slap on a few quick years can apply as much to an established garden as to a brand new site. The land may have been 'in cultivation' for decades but have grown little other than perennial and bedding plants. Perhaps there is nothing more than ground cover, or the previous owners merely planted trees and cut the grass.

Each of these gardens will adapt well to short-cut techniques but there are degrees of corner-cutting – from instant gardening to

more subtle, medium-term actions. So, before you start, you need first to decide just how 'short cut' you want your garden to be.

What is your timespan? Do you want to drag your garden round in a single season? If your house is about to go on sale, the chances are you do. But if you are not planning a quick move, and you are blessed with at least a modicum of patience, perhaps you will be more content with a hybrid of instant gardening for quick effect, backed up with longer term – and therefore, more permanent – planting and design projects. Perhaps the ideal, short-cut or otherwise, is to aim to achieve a garden that looks good almost at once but will go on getting better and better.

KEEPING UP APPEARANCES

However gorgeous a garden may be, maintenance will always be a crucial factor in design and planting policy. Leisure is more plentiful now than it was in the great gardening years of the early nineteen hundreds, but few modern families would take kindly to the idea of laborious chores every weekend, so they need to be kept to the minimum.

At the design stage decide just how much time you will want to spare, and plan accordingly. Vegetables, formal bedding displays and large numbers of containers take more looking after than do shrubs or ground cover. Lawns need regular mowing and occasional feeding. Roses need pruning and keeping free of disease. Some perennials need dividing every year and annuals need sowing. It may be imprudent to opt for all these activities, but a proportion of them will be necessary if your garden is to be truly interesting and productive.

Some of the short-cut techniques that are described in this book involve a greater level of maintenance than conventional gardens normally require. Others need a special effort at first, when they are being set up and while they get established, but will be labour saving in the long run, once their construction and planting have been completed.

ABOVE *The right balance between the paving, container and pond edge and their sympathetic furnishing of shrubs and herbaceous plants has been struck here. Plants alone will not make a garden design work and hard materials without artistic planting make for a sterile view.*

2

DEFINING THE SHORT-CUT GARDEN

Crusty professionals like to point out that in gardening there are no short cuts. Patience is the key to success, they insist, and all you need to do to acquire the magnificence of the historic gardens of the world, is first plant and then, like everyone in the film *Casablanca*, you wait. And wait. And wait!

In some respects they are right, but this chapter suggests alternative approaches to gardening that will enable you to create a fine garden far more quickly than you would have dreamt possible. It shows how some gardens, for example a formal or kitchen style, can be set up instantly (pages 16–21). Others, an architectural or informal design for instance, may take a little longer to establish but can still look good meanwhile (pages 22–27). Yet others, such as a woodland or cottage style, require more effort at the beginning but are easier to maintain (pages 28–35).

Backed by a mellow brick wall, massed vegetation gives this garden a sense of age even though many of the plants and containers are recent additions.

THE INSTANT GARDEN

PROTECT PLANTS
Screen vulnerable plants from wind

PACKED LOOK
Grow plants close together

FILL IN GAPS
Replace any casualties

BRIGHTEN UP WITH BULBS
Plant in autumn for spring colour

SPEEDY COVER
Select vigorous climbers

OLD MATERIALS
Second-hand goods are already mellowed

Patience may be a virtue but, as far as gardening is concerned, it can hardly be a vice to say 'I want it now', especially if you know you may not be in the same place in the next year or two.

Creating a garden in a single season can present something of a challenge, particularly if it begins on a building site with tortured topsoil and builder's rubble everywhere, but it can be done, and done convincingly with more than just a splurge of colourful annual bedding plants. The two-year garden is more easily achievable.

The only way to achieve convincing results is by taking short cuts – that is, by deploying a series of strategies to hasten development. The formal garden (pages 18–19) and the kitchen garden (pages 20–21) are two successful short-term gardens based on such strategies.

SPEEDY PLANTS

As far as plants are concerned, the first consideration to guarantee the shortest cuts is to make sure that they are all growing at their maximum safe speed.

▶ To achieve a rapid cover begin planting as early in the season as is practicable, and ensure that your plants are going into the most favourable conditions possible.

▶ Crowd your garden with fast-growing large plants that will contribute lots of maturity after only a couple of seasons.

▶ In the early days, a generous and speedy cover is your main objective. Ignore the conventional rules which advise you to space your plants to allow for several years' growth. Pack them in instead.

▶ Be prepared to thin plants out, even before the end of the first season. Growth rates vary from year to year but in a warm, moist summer, growth will be more exuberant than average.

Outline trees should not be packed together, of course – unless you want to create a thick, wind-resisting screen. Most of your garden trees will have been selected for their intrinsic beauty, or for their distinctive shapes and profile, and should not be masked by overcrowding.

▶ For vertical cover, concentrate on the most rapid-growing species to guarantee early dividends. Rampaging climbers such as *Clematis montana* or *Akebia quinata* cover walls or trellis much more quickly than the more sedate varieties of climbing rose or large-flowered clematis hybrids. Of course, there is plenty of scope for planting these more elegant species and varieties as well, but they take a little longer to come into their own.

Resist the temptation of going for maximum speed at any price, however. Invasive climbers such as Russian vine (*Polygonum baldschuanicum* syn. *Fallopia baldschuanica*) may give you a swift cover but within a short time it will have smothered everything else.

▶ The quickest plants of all are summer annuals and bedding. Although it would be quite wrong to rely exclusively on such instant gardening, bedding is likely to provide the best of the colour in the first season, so you cannot afford to leave it out altogether.

► Plug unexpected gaps, perhaps where there have been losses, with selected tender plants.

► Where new shrubs are too small to make much of a statement in year one, try introducing some big, tender plants like standard abutilons, some of the shrubby salvias such as *S. involucrata* 'Bethellii' or even standard fuchsias. These swell the vegetation and boost the colour content.

► Plant big drifts of colourful tender perennials in a wide mixed border for instant effect. Such plants as *Argyranthemum frutescens* are rapid developers of great beauty, coming in a wide range of pastel shades including pink, pale yellow and white. The peacock blue *Salvia patens* and the very large-flowered penstemons also make superb instant plants. Look especially for the mauve *Penstemon* 'Alice Hindley' and the scarlet 'King George' and plant them with some of the more leafy pot geranium varieties for a vivid display in an astonishingly short time.

► Take cuttings of all these tender perennials. They root in a matter of days to provide an abundance of young plants which can be over-wintered for the following season. Alternatively, you can buy fresh each year.

► If you move to a new home in autumn, spring bulbs are a spectacular way of taking a short cut to colour. Daffodils, tulips, crocuses and all the other little gems that brighten up the gloomy days of late winter will give a bright display, quickly. If, in subsequent years, you find you have overdone it, don't worry. Bulbs are easy to remove and re-plant at almost any time of year.

► To ensure a mellow look in the first year, select old building materials whenever possible. Flagstones, secondhand bricks and even old concrete paving slabs look far more attractive from day one than when new. With care, it is possible to lay bricks and blocks with much of the moss and lichen still intact.

ABOVE *Cramming herbaceous perennials and annuals in front of young shrubs in a border gives an instant packed look. As the shrubs mature, the gap fillers can be removed as necessary.*

OPPOSITE *Planted in the autumn, bulbs are a sure way of providing welcome colour just a few months later. They can be left in the ground to multiply and spread naturally.*

FORMAL GARDEN SHORT CUTS

▶Lavender and santolina have been selected to provide colour and fragrance as well as a speedy hedge. New plants should grow strongly in their first year but will need severe clipping immediately after flowering if they are to form a dense hedge.

SPEEDY HEDGES
Plant fast growers among slower ones

INSTANT TOPIARY
Train ivy round frames

POTS OF FORMALITY
Large containers add style

ACCENTUATE OUTLINE
Erect formal fencing

CREATE A FOCAL POINT
Install a garden seat

MATURE CLIPPED SHRUBS
A good investment for containers

The geometric layout and topiary shapes of the traditional formal garden (above) are achievable in a very short time (right).

Formal planting depends on geometry. In most gardens, hard structures such as walls and buildings provide the beginnings, but the theme of curves, angles and symmetrical patterns can also be developed with plants.

You can hasten the development of a formal framework by alternating slow-growing, traditional evergreen box or yew hedging with a simple pattern of faster growing hedge. You can also achieve a finished look that much more quickly by judicious siting of seats and containers. Place containers with great deliberation, to punctuate pathways or accompany seats or benches. A large pot, or two, furnished with bold-foliaged hostas, can effect an instant transformation. Containers planted with fairly mature shrubs can sometimes be purchased, at a price, but using rapid climbers such as ivy trained round frameworks to look like topiary can provide quick results far more cheaply.

Most evergreen hedges need at least an annual clip and often look better for two. But slow-growing shrubs, if you have selected the right kind, will look after themselves and need little attention, apart from the occasional trim to remove dead or damaged pieces. The fast-growing hedging will begin to age after a few seasons and need replacing every five years.

▶The centre beds feature combinations of heliotrope with marigold and balm with golden balm, surrounded by *Lavandula* 'Hidcote' and *Santolina neapolitana* 'Sulphurea'. The pots contain bay and trained ivy. Antirrhinums are prominent in the perimeter bed.

▶The low, white picket fence provides a substantial shape. The plants behind are selected for speed and flower-power so that they will dominate the display within a few weeks of planting. Standard plants by the seat add more height and increase the volume of living material.

Timespan Two growing seasons
Life expectancy Fast-growing hedges, up to five years; evergreens indefinite
Work can be phased to suit budget and time available

▶ Gravel paths are the cheapest choice but extra maturity is possible with old materials such as used paving slabs or second-hand bricks.

▶ Set at key points, containers provide instant structure and quick maturity. Containers must go well with their surroundings but should contrast strongly enough to make a positive statement. The bigger they are, the greater the impact and, to heighten the effect, they should be planted with mature specimens.

▶ Topiary takes a long time to take shape but rapid climbers such as ivy can be trained to grow over wire frames, giving a hedging-like effect. To maintain the desired formal shape and to avoid a ragged appearance, climbers grown this way will need to be tied in frequently, rather than clipped.

▶ Within the beds, a strong colour scheme with rapid plants helps to dilute the newness and rawness of the layout. Perennial foliage plants like balm and golden balm can be clipped level for formality.

KITCHEN GARDEN SHORT CUTS

▶ Holes made by harvesting crops should be filled immediately with replacement plants, ensuring continuity of production, and continuing to build on the mature effect that a dense plant cover gives.

▶ To ensure maximum growth rates, woven hurdles have been used to reduce wind speed and make a cosy environment. As the plants develop, they will also tend to shelter each other, especially where planting is dense.

ACCESSIBILITY
Include plenty of paths

RAPID CROPS
Some mature in a few weeks

GROW UP
Train crops up supports or arches

DECORATIVE PLANTING
Choose attractive vegetables

USEFUL SCREENS
Train fruit espaliers

INTRODUCE SHAPE
Plant ballerina apples

The long-established look of a symmetrically laid out kitchen garden (above) can be attained remarkably quickly (right).

A kitchen garden is so much more than just a vegetable patch. Well planned, it can combine beauty with utility, providing a constant supply of vegetables and fruit as well as flowers for cutting.

As with a formal garden, a geometric layout looks better in a kitchen garden and makes management easier than an informal scheme would. Beds should be arranged so that all parts can be reached from the path.

Structure, too, is an important consideration. Well-designed arches and supports, for instance, will look good from the moment they are erected. Decorative arches can support climbing food crops, from melons or squashes to grape vines or kiwi fruit, as well as carry beautiful climbers like wisterias or roses. Walls, arches and hedges all help to check wind speed and thus improve shelter. You can also train fruit trees in cordons or espaliers around the edge of a kitchen garden to double as food sources and decorative screens.

Kitchen gardens can be decoratively planted. Most vegetables have their colourful variants and ordinary, well-grown vegetables have their own special charm – carrots, with their ferny foliage and the glaucous blue of young cabbages are fine examples, and the flowers and leaves of the globe artichoke are handsome enough to grace the smartest of flower borders.

▶ A kitchen garden benefits from a year-round succession of flowers, not just for cutting but also to heighten the colour outdoors: daffodils, tulips, Dutch iris, florist's anemones and pansies in spring; pinks, asters, sweet peas and roses in summer; chrysanthemums in autumn; and Christmas roses, snowdrops and sweet violets in winter.

▶ With so much coming and going as crops develop and are harvested, it is important to retain structure in the layout with more permanent plants at strategic places. Purple sage and other herbs fulfil this function at corners and along paths.

Timespan One season
Life expectancy Vegetables, one season
Fruit and ornamentals vary from three seasons to a decade or more

▶Fast-growing climbing plants such as runner beans, trained here on cane wigwams, and squashes or marrows, which can be trained onto a frame or pergola, provide the quickest height.

▶Height is important for shape and winter outline. Espalier fruit trees take a while to mature but, here, the rigid stems of ballerina apples provide quick height and form. Purchased as two- or three-year-old plants, they will fruit in their first season.

THE LONG-TERM GARDEN

DOUBLE PLANT
Rapid shrubs alongside slower ones

DRESS THE GARDEN
Strategic statues and containers

PROVIDE STRUCTURE
Erect balustrading, blockwork, pergolas or trellis

ABUNDANT ANNUALS
Sow in autumn and spring

POP IN EXTRAS
Fill gaps with spare or bought plants

ABOVE *Cool foliage themes using silver, grey and pale greens create a restful effect with a young whitebeam tree presiding over lady's mantle, pearl everlasting and the variegated grass* Holcus mollis. *The sedum will flower later, adding a touch of pink and attracting late summer butterflies.*

OPPOSITE *Shrubs take a few seasons to get established but while they develop the spaces between them provide planting opportunities for medium-term perennials. Here, candelabra primulas and* Primula viallii *make a colourful foreground planting.*

Gardening is about much more than merely the short term. One of its chief pleasures is to watch, year by year, the progress of the trees, shrubs and plant associations, changing the whole ambience of the environment.

Even when fully developed, no garden is static. There is constant change not only as things grow, mature and age, but as the gardener's ideas change, too. Gardens last a lifetime. Great gardens last considerably longer.

All very well, you might think, for those who have the time. For sure, we want it to be wonderful fifteen years hence, but what can we do to make what is now a bare site pleasurable to wander through tomorrow? Today? The answer is, quite a lot.

In the garden's early stages, the slowest growing plants, chosen for their superior contribution as mature plants, may not make much impact. So the target is a kind of interim solution, a bogus maturity while you wait for the real thing. This is quite feasible, as the architectural garden (pages 24–25) and the informal garden (pages 26–27) show. But you may become so fond of some of the instant measures that you decide to let them become permanent features. If this happens, you might want to revise some of your original long-term plans, so be flexible in your thinking!

▶ To develop an outline quickly, introduce plants that provide big shapes fast while the more permanent ones grow to size. Thus, while desirable evergreen shrubs and trees, such as yew, box or holly are settling in, you could interplant them with large grasses perhaps, or rapid shrubs like buddleias, or even with outsize perennials such as angelica, *Rheum palmatum* or *Inula magnifica.*

▶ You will need to make your initial plantings far denser than would normally be recommended in a conventional garden, but your longer term subjects, if they are to reach potential size, will need *lebensraum*, so that they can develop without having to undergo restrictive pruning or training. Therefore, be prepared to thin out after the first couple of seasons to make space.

▶ Select rapid plants not just for their speed but to integrate happily into the over-all planting, even if you intend to remove them after a few seasons. Make sure they do not threaten the lives of the slower plants. Bright annuals, for example, are fine unless their colours scream at the more permanent plants.

►A number of annuals make better plants which flower for much longer if they are sown in autumn rather than in spring. Sow half in autumn and half in spring to lengthen their flowering time.

►Go for speedy gap fillers. In the early years of a new garden, you may be spending more on plants than you bargained for, but while the shrubs and permanent plants spread themselves, the gaps will yawn, especially in summer, unless they are crammed with rapid-growing temporary plants. Tender perennials are ideal for this, as are hardy annuals which flower within a single season from seed sown into the ground.

►One single container, strategically placed, can transform the scene. It creates a resting point for the eye; it makes shadows; it adds character. A large pot with a thoughtfully composed arrangement of flowering plants standing at the end of a path, for example, is a pleasing feature – one which you can set up in a single afternoon after a brief visit to the garden centre!

►Design of the container can be important and the golden rule is, if in doubt, go for bigger and higher. Large containers are better from the practical point of view since they are more efficient at retaining moisture and allow their occupants to grow bigger and therefore flower for longer.

►Group containers into instant gardens; they can become as permanent as you like, and can be changed or re-arranged from time to time to suit different plants at different seasons.

►Use statuary to create an instant garden scene – amusing, tranquil or contemplative, but always interesting.

►Provide speedy structure and form by erecting various kinds of balustrading, fancy blockwork, pergolas and trellis. Take care not to overdo things or you could end up with what looks like a garden accessories store.

'ARCHITECTURAL' SHORT CUTS

▶ Architectural planting works best if it is part of a good garden design. Structures here, including the pathway, climbing frame, little stone bridge and furniture, all play an important role in providing the ideal setting for the plants. Once installed, these permanent fixtures maintain the structure while the plants develop.

▶ Plants featured in this garden include *Ligularia dentata* 'Desdemona', *Anemone × hybrida* and *Vitis coignetiae*.

THINK BIG
Select plants with outsize leaves

DISTINCT SHAPES
Bold foliage and spiky plants

MOVEMENT AND SOUND
Graceful grasses and bamboo

SOFTEN HARD LINES
Climbers and ground covers

LARGE CONTAINERS
Mature plants or fast growers in pots

SPRING BULBS
Colour for the dormant season

The basic ingredients of a classic architectural garden (above) can be brought together in a relatively short time (right).

An architectural garden, even one which bristles with man-made artifacts, depends heavily on architectural plants. Structures like walls, steps, archways, formal terraces and so on are merely architectural hardware and cannot be assembled as a garden without their furnishings of plants. Pergolas, the sides of buildings and dividing fences all cry out for climbers. The harsh edges of wall footings need to be softened, steps to be given character and paving brought to life by the addition of plants.

As for the plants themselves, the term 'architectural' is generally used to denote distinctiveness of shape – bold foliage, spiky leaves, tall and graceful stems. Most of the classic architectural plants take a few seasons to develop but there are other, quicker species that can be used in conjunction with them. Ultimately, these faster, coarser plants may outlive their usefulness and warrant expulsion.

One of the drawbacks of so much man-made structure is that it can be rigid and lifeless. Besides bamboos, there are faster-growing plants which are important because they introduce movement. The taller grasses such as *Spartina pectinata* or *Miscanthus purpurascens* grow huge in a season and are full of movement. Other good grasses and grass-like plants include the golden oat (*Stipa gigantea*), *Cortaderia selloana* and the graceful oatgrass (*Helictotrichon sempervirens*).

▶ Plants provide living architecture in this garden. Herbaceous species with large, bold foliage highlight the path edge but are interplanted with background greenery. Large-leaved climbers give height but also make a strong statement.

▶ Many architectural plants, particularly large herbaceous species, are only effective for part of the year. It is important to extend the architectural effect to all seasons by including plants such as bulbs or winter shrubs. In any case, the garden will depend more heavily on man-made structures and trees for its architecture during winter.

▶ A strategically placed container, planted with a mature abutilon for speed, plays a strong architectural role. Any climbing plant of a tall frame and a pleasing outline would work almost as well.

Timespan One growing season, mature in three
Life expectancy Indefinite

►The Japanese feel of this layout is reinforced by grasses and bamboos which, as well as adding height, bring the planting to life with their grace and movement.

►Spiky foliage in the stream, provided by irises and reed mace, is reflected in the water, doubling its effectiveness and contrasting with the flat, round water lily leaves.

INFORMAL GARDEN SHORT CUTS

▶ Big, exotic-looking herbaceous plants, with their giant leaves or distinctive flowers, or just by their huge stature, imbue a border with character. Planted apart and according to their increasing height, they soon spread to cram surrounding space with ample lushness, softening the edges of the path.

▶ Clockwise from centre left, plants include: bergenia, *Rheum*, Madonna lilies, *Osmanthus*, *Physocarpus opulifolius* 'Dart's Gold', *Inula magnifica*, bronze fennel, *Salix exigua*, *Salvia uliginosa*, *Fagus sylvatica* 'Dawyck Purple', *Cupressus macrocarpa* 'Goldcrest', *Rosa* 'Albertine', clematis, eucalyptus, *Buddleia davidii* 'Pink Delight', *Chrysanthemum uliginosum*, gunnera, angelica, *Choisya ternata*, *Hosta* 'Royal Standard'.

FAST-GROWING CLIMBERS
Grow climbers up garden structures to gain height

INTERIM TREES
Grow fast-growing trees until slower ones mature

TEMPORARY SHRUBS
Plant rampant shrubs for fast shape and structure

EXOTIC PERENNIALS
Outsize perennials add maturity to a border

COLOURFUL INFILL
Let self-seeding annuals fill gaps between shrubs

The sense of long-established informality (above) can be reproduced quickly using a few artful devices (right).

The informal garden is really no more than a little piece of natural landscape – the country-side in microcosm. All the best aspects of the wild are brought in: attractive curves, natural-looking tree-scapes and mixed borders where colour regimes, if any, are gently imposed to keep everything looking as it would in the wild. Any water features also imitate nature with meandering streams, waterfalls and asymme-trically shaped ponds; the boundary between wet and dry areas should be softly defined, ideally as a boggy or marshy piece of ground.

Artificial structures are usually kept to a minimum. Functional constructions such as terraces, gateways or steps are bound to be there, but where an architectural garden, for instance, relies on building works to give it shape, an informal garden uses plants instead. This is not to say, however, that all gardens with arches or pergolas are formal, or that gardens which only use plants are informal.

In terms of short-cut gardening, creating instant maturity in an informal garden presents special problems. Whereas man-made struc-tures can effect an instant transformation, trees take time and, while buildings remain exactly as they are, they grow and change shape, altering the proportions. In winter, when rapid-growing perennials and colourful annuals have all died away, a void is left in their place.

Timespan Two growing seasons, mature in five
Life expectancy Indefinite

▶ A pleasing backdrop, providing year-round interest, can soon be created using a mixture of fast-growing evergreen and deciduous trees.

▶ A grassy path meanders invitingly through curvaceous, packed borders, making the most of the many different plants. Grass can be quickly laid using turf, or it will mature from seed in just one season.

▶ Sited at the end of the path, an old seat nestling in an arbour draped with fast climbers instils a long-established feel. This arresting focal point provided interest before the trees grew to their present height.

▶ Shrubs create lovely, informal, undulating mounds of foliage and blossom. Fast-growing ones can be used until more choice, slower species planted nearby mature; the coarser shrubs are then moved elsewhere or discarded.

THE LOW-MAINTENANCE GARDEN

ESTABLISH THE SHAPE
Lay pathways and surfaces first

VERSATILE GROUND COVER
Try many different kinds

USE BIENNIALS
Free-seeding foxgloves, mulleins, honesty and wallflowers colonize rapidly

MULTIPLYING BULBS
Choose rapidly increasing types

LONG GRASS
Leave corners or patches undisturbed for wildlife cover

ABOVE *Requiring little attention, lavender, thyme and other plants that thrive in dry conditions are perfect companions for paving in the low-maintenance garden. Old-style paving slabs, whether natural stone or composition, mellow quickly and look better once plants have softened the hard edges.*

OPPOSITE *Perennials, including lady's mantle, brunneras and Helleborus argutifolius, have flowed over a shaded path giving a feeling of establishment even though the planting is comparatively recent. The foxglove looks as though it was a volunteer arrival – a happy event in the low-maintenance garden.*

The short-cut gardens described so far will be impressive very quickly, at a price. Instant planting can be costly, especially when mature trees and shrubs are used and when massed bedding is planted. There is also cost in terms of labour. Formal gardens with bedding and kitchen gardens demand constant tending so, if you love gardening but your time is at a premium, it may be more sensible to aim for a speedy garden which needs minimum maintenance once it is established.

Though hardly 'instant' in their early stages – low-maintenance gardens may actually be harder work at first than more conventional ones – there are almost as many effective short-cut strategies for low-maintenance gardens as for more short-term and intermediate ones.

The totally maintenance-free garden is, of course, a myth. Any area in which plants are cultivated needs some husbandry. Even the wildest, most dishevelled properties require a

certain level of management, be they plantsmen's paradises or naturalists' wildlife habitats. My definition of low-maintenance garden, here, is one where routine jobs are minimized rather than eliminated.

As with everything else in life, you tend to get out what you put in. Therefore, a low-maintenance garden is never likely to look quite as ravishing as one which is lovingly groomed day by day. However, with a bit of low cunning, you would be surprised at how much you can get away with.

Clearly, it is easier to make an informal garden labour saving than a formal one, which would have hedges to clip, and spring and summer bedding to change. With an informal layout, the lines will be softer and less distinct: there will be sweeping curves and probably bulges or irregularities in the borders. Grass may be longer or rougher, and, therefore, in need of fewer cuts per year. Large areas of the garden can be left, more or less, to look after themselves. Such ploys have been incorporated in the woodland garden (pages 32–33) and the cottage garden (pages 34–35).

The secret of success in the low-maintenance garden lies in a combination of design and planting. The planting takes time to gel and at first, you may wonder why everything seems to be so much trouble. But if the planting has been well thought out and the design is fault-free, the garden will settle within a couple of seasons, and gradually you will be able to take more of a back seat.

DESIGN CONSIDERATIONS

It depends what you want, of course, but certain design elements can make a huge difference to the amount of time spent working in the garden once it is established.

▶ **Man-made structures help to provide a backbone. Informal planting can appear to be a little formless and untidy but a garden which has a clear-cut design with such structures as pergolas, walls or screens feels more cohesive than one which has been set out and planted on an *ad hoc* basis.**

▶ **Paving is virtually maintenance free, but it is inclined to be hard and unwelcoming unless softened by planting. Plant at least along its edges but preferably all over – in cracks and planting spaces.**

▶ **When laying paving, incorporate crevices or small beds, to accommodate plants that will soften up the hard lines.**

▶ **Gravel is a cheap surface requiring minimal maintenance to keep it clear of weeds. It lends itself equally well to formal and informal gardening, and can be used in pathways or on terraces, planted or not planted.**

▶ **Although grass is not necessarily low maintenance – close-mown lawns are hard work and flower meadows need even more careful looking after – if well planned it can enhance other plantings. For large areas, the ride-on mower makes life easy.**

▶**Arrange a low-maintenance under-planting around trees on grass that have low-hanging branches, so that they seldom or never need mowing under.**

TIME-SAVING PLANTING

Choice of plants is important, but not half so much as how and where you plant them. The basis of the planting plan in a low-maintenance garden is to make the plants do as much of the work for you as possible.

Maintenance problems often arise simply because of plants which need too much molly-coddling or which outgrow and swamp their neighbours. Even the most knowledgeable plantsman makes mistakes and for the rest of us, there is no knowing how a plant will behave until we have tried it. It is probably better, therefore, not to be restrictive on what we introduce into the garden – the last thing we want is to miss good plant opportunities – but to keep new introductions under the closest observation until they have settled down and we know exactly how they will behave.

▶**Ground cover plays a key role, obviously. It is available in a vast array of colours and types, so plant lots of it.**

▶**Underplant outline trees with low shrubs and understorey plants that will both delight you in their seasons and help to maintain a healthy mantle of plant life over the soil at other times.**

Mixed borders need to be filled out with self-perpetuating colonies of plants, all associating well, with no single species making itself a nuisance by threatening the others. To achieve this, a border needs to develop a kind of balance, but that can take years to reach. In the short-cut garden, we may not have time for such long-term plans but there are strategies that will help the planting to establish itself quickly. There are plenty of bulbous plants which provide a speedy show for very little investment, and which, with minimal attention, keep quietly multiplying and spreading over the years.

The dividing line between a plant that is invasive and a 'good doer' is a thin one, however, so avoid introducing plants which are likely to become troublesome. *Campanula*

rapunculoides and sweet cicely (*Myrrhis odorata*) – both lovely plants in the right place – are far too thuggishly invasive to let loose in a small garden, for instance.

▶**Use self-seeders and spreaders. In the short-cut garden, plants which self seed or spread rapidly into self-maintaining colonies are invaluable. Foxgloves seed copiously but are seldom difficult to remove if they have spread too far. Honesty (*Lunaria biennis*) is similar, scattering its seedlings everywhere but it looks charming in spring.**

▶**Select bulbs which bulk up. *Chionodoxa luciliae*, *C. sardensis*, *Scilla sibirica*, most crocus species – especially *C. tommasinianus* – and *Anemone blanda* are all examples of small bulbs that multiply well, both by seed and vegetatively. On a slightly larger scale, wild daffodils (*Narcissus pseudonarcissus*) or their more vigorous hybrids, such as 'February Gold', the summer snowflake (*Leucojum aestivum*) and larger fritillaries, particularly the crown imperial (*Fritillaria imperialis*), go on steadily increasing for years without needing attention.**

ABOVE *A wild garden, such as this damp meadow of typical European wetland flora, may be difficult to establish but, once the balance between species has been struck, it should almost manage itself.*

OPPOSITE *Rampaging shrubs such as buddleia and tree mallow, backed up by a thick planting of perennials have all but blocked out weeds. The key to minimal maintenance is establishing a dense plant cover.*

WOODLAND GARDEN SHORT CUTS

CONDITION THE SOIL
Add leaf mould or peat

RAPID SPREADERS
Begin with vigorous species; thin out later

LAISSEZ-FAIRE
Fallen leaves and branches enhance the scene

SIMPLE FLOWERS
Introduce wild species and small-flowered cultivars

THICK UNDERGROWTH
Provide cover for wildlife

The magical timelessness of a mature woodland walk (above) can be reproduced easily in a garden where there are trees (right).

To succeed, a woodland garden has to be well ordered. What you are creating, in effect, is a small pocket of wild landscape in a garden setting. As such, it will always need some management input and, even though there may not be much physical hard work once it has become established, getting the right set-up will take both skill and patience.

For a natural look, plants must be fruitful and multiply by themselves. Artificial planting, even if carried out with extreme sensitivity, tends to show, whereas natural self-seeding, the bulking up of bulbs and the creeping of rootstocks to form mats of mixed species, all help to create the desired effect. But such an effect takes time, and a certain amount of unevenness is inevitable in the first seasons.

Although purists may insist on native plants, a well-planned woodland garden can carry exotic wild species and even certain hybrids without losing its natural look. The secret is to use plants which give the impression of being wild – plants with small, simple flowers and foliage which is not abnormally marked.

In the wild, woodland plants grow where there is a natural covering of leaf litter. In an artificial wild garden, such plants as primroses, trilliums and epimediums grow better with plenty of organic matter in the soil. Fertilizer will ruin the character of wild flowers.

▶ There are no hard lines. The pathway is little more than a suggestion of where to walk, with stepping stones set into the ground at intervals, but it is positive enough to lead the eye into a bewitching middle distance. What structure there is has been provided by the trees and shrubs.

▶ A 'fallen' tree trunk helps to foster a woodsy atmosphere but other features such as old roots or stumps left behind after felling trees would serve just as well. Logs often decay very slowly over many years and crop interesting fungi and lichens as they go.

▶ Most of the plants used are wild – woodland species from different parts of the world. European ajuga, for example, looks quite at home with American trilliums or with Asian meconopsis. Where garden cultivars are introduced, these should be simple and look uncultivated, as with the small narcissus illustrated here.

▶ A woodland garden needs to be wildlife friendly. The undergrowth here is allowed to grow thickly; ground cover around the log is disturbed as little as possible and some insect food plants are included among the plantings.

Timespan Two growing seasons
Life expectancy Indefinite

▶Advantage has been taken of existing mature trees to create a woodland atmosphere. The soil has been enriched with leaf mould or peat, and woodland plants have been encouraged to spread. Much of the foliage can be allowed to lie where it falls in autumn.

▶Sweet violets, old-fashioned primroses, *Helleborus orientalis*, *Narcissus* 'Geranium', bluebells and *Narcissus* 'Thalia' lend their charm to this woodland garden.

COTTAGE GARDEN SHORT CUTS

RANDOM PLANTING

Large groups create a riotous effect

CONTROL COLOUR

Keep shade combinations in order

ENSURE CONTINUITY

Select plants that peak at different times

PROVIDE STRUCTURE

Rapid ramblers for height

TRADITIONAL PLANTS

Evoke an old-fashioned feel

SOW ANNUALS IN AUTUMN

Ensure early cover the following year

USE CLIMBERS

To scramble over shrubs and up trees

The random planting of perennials with mixed colours and crowded stems of the mature cottage garden (above) soon can be reproduced (right).

Originally, cottage gardens were utilitarian rather than decorative. There would be pigs and chickens as well as vegetables and herbs. Nowadays, ornament is more often the chief objective but it is quite possible to combine beauty with use and grow a modest number of vegetables, even in a small cottage garden.

The more riotous the planting, the more successful the cottage garden seems to be. But despite the apparently haphazard approach, a cottage garden does need order. Colours, or rather, colour combinations have to be considered, especially where large-flowered plants are used. There are practical considerations, too. It would be foolhardy to plant invasive annuals, for instance, so that they swamp the spring primroses and violets. If all the tall plants grew at the front, they would mask lower ones at the back. In short, the skill in cottage planting is being able to tread that thin line between relaxed informality and chaos.

After a few years, the cottage garden may well grow out of hand and need a complete overhaul. The outline or skeleton planting should have been so well planned from the beginning that it can stay put for good, but the rest of the plants can be ripped out and then replanted or discarded. The chances are, shrubs and other plants will have grown at differing rates and will need either severe pruning or rearranging. In spite of the drastic treatment, the rejuvenated cottage garden will look perfect in its first new season.

▶ Flowers have been chosen to harmonize with their background. A period cottage looks best if the garden in front is planted with distinctly old-fashioned plants. Colours tend to be soft and flower sizes small. A modern house, with stark materials such as new brick can carry stronger colours in its foreground, as long as they do not clash.

▶ Among the plants gracing this garden are achillea, *Geranium psilostemon*, lupins, eschscholzia, delphiniums, marigolds, *Papaver orientale*, rue and lavender.

Timespan One growing season
Life expectancy Three or four seasons, renewable

►The old apple tree, an existing feature, has made a pretty backdrop to the planting and, as well as being productive, has constant beauty with blossom in spring, colourful fruit and good winter outline. In the absence of such a feature, a climbing frame could be constructed and furnished with a mix of rambling roses.

►Traditional cottager's plants such as alecost, skirret and old-fashioned flowers like lavender and pinks mature quickly to flower in their first season and also give the garden an authentic old cottage appearance.

►Rapid rambling roses such as 'Albertine', 'New Dawn' or 'Albéric Barbier' or even more vigorous shrub roses provide colour earlier than roses which grow at a more sedate pace.

►The essence of a cottage garden is random planting. But, to avoid the dull gap that can follow the early summer crescendo, care is needed in selecting plants that are at their best at different seasons. Here, perennials such as lupins, valerian and pinks can be cut back after their first flush and will flower again.

3

FIRST
STEPS TO
SHORT
CUTS

The types of short cuts you will want to take in your
garden will, of course, depend on its state. Someone
who has just moved into a newly built house, for
instance, faces a different set of circumstances from
someone wishing to make a quick impression on an
existing garden. The first thing to do is to take stock
of what is there and build on that.

Sites vary enormously in their natural attributes, of
course, but even if your patch seems so hopeless as to
make gardening impossible, do not despair. You will
be surprised, and delighted, at what even the most
unpromising plot can be made to do!

As plants need ideal growing conditions to thrive
and grow at rapid rates, poor soil and environment can
be improved to give plants a head start. Existing
features, even ones that may not seem promising at
first sight, can be incorporated to hurry along a sense
of maturity.

*The well-sheltered environment
provided by a vegetation-covered
boundary has paid dividends in
this successful garden.*

ASSESSING EXISTING FEATURES

ABOVE *Rock plants such as arabis, aubrieta and yellow* Alyssum saxatile, *which have been allowed to seed, creating a cascade of bright colour, have transformed dull concrete steps.*

Sometimes it is necessary to give a garden a thorough overhaul. As a new owner, you may dislike the original design or planting and want to make changes, or the garden may have become so overgrown that there is little that can be done short of a total renovation. Even where there is a good collection of trees accompanied by well-made structures and mature under-plantings, that special feeling of maturity or stature may still have evaded the site.

Fortunately, there are several useful short-cut strategies for maximizing existing features. And, where necessary, it can be more fun to put a ruinous garden to rights than to create a new one from a bare site.

The one advantage a neglected garden usually has is maturity. So, however profound the renovation has to be, it will be worth trying to preserve some of that precious maturity. The same goes when making alterations in any garden, whatever its stage of development. Careful evaluation before taking any drastic action can result in a prime short cut to a great garden, even if most of the planting is new.

TAKE STOCK OF TREES

As trees take so many years to develop, they do more than any other feature to give a garden an impression of age. Any tree, even an ugly one or an unremarkable species, needs to be carefully evaluated, not just in the light of where it stands now, but how it would fit into a revised design. Consider every tree in the garden before making a decision about its future. For the sake of the maturity trees impart, and their import-ance for outline, adjust design to accommodate them if necessary. Once a tree has been felled, the action is irreversible, so think long and hard and, if in doubt, leave it alone until you are really sure.

▶ **If an old leaning tree has an interesting outline, rather than chop it down try propping it up. Use a substantial support, or more than one if necessary, but make sure that the tree is safe; take professional advice if in doubt.**

Putting a value on a tree is not always easy. It may be that the location of the tree is more important than its type. A group of conifers that have become too large for their surroundings, for example, may be worth tolerating because they block off the prevailing wind or mask an unsightly structure or view beyond. A gnarled apple tree on a lawn may be past its optimum crop-bearing age but is too cherished to let go.

▶ **Where a tree or shrub is beyond redemption and earmarked for removal, you need not fell it straight away, especially if it is to be replaced by a younger specimen. If you can, plant the replacement nearby and allow it to deve-lop for one, two or more seasons before removing the condemned tree – which meanwhile continues to contribute matur-ity. The point at which to cull is when the old plants are beginning to inhibit the development of the new introductions.**

THE ART OF PRUNING

Trees that are selected for preservation will probably need attention. Indeed, you may not be able to make your final decision about whether to keep or fell them until you have seen how they look tidied up. Pruning is a

SAVE TREES
Preserve mature specimens

PRUNE TO IMPROVE
Transform trees and shrubs

REVITALIZE SHRUBS
Cut back to the ground

CAPITALIZE ON SUCKERS
Create new shrubs

COVER UP
Disguise ugly features with climbers

SHORT-TERM PLANTS
Use quick growers until finer, slower ones mature

CORRECT ERRORS
Replant where necessary

technique which anyone can develop with practice, but cleaning up a mature tree may call for the skills of a qualified tree surgeon. If you are inexperienced, but feel inclined to try pruning an old tree yourself, refer to one of the many excellent works on arboriculture before you start. If there are any unimportant specimens in the garden, practise on those first!

Many species of woody plant respond positively to drastic pruning. Often, shrubs which have become huge and entangled, perhaps collapsing under their own weight, can be cut almost to ground level. Their vast root systems ensure that within a single season they will have put out vigorous new growths which will flower profusely the following year. Conifers, with the notable exception of yew, suffer from such action and frequently die when cut back to brown wood.

▶ **Prune eyesore shrubs, that have become much too big, to the ground. Buddleias, camellias, viburnums, roses, *Rubus*, *Weigela*, *Kolkwitzia* and cotoneasters all** respond well to such brutality. **Most of the more rapid rhododendrons — especially those raised from *Rhododendron ponticum* — will also take it, as will the majority of broad-leaved evergreens.**

There may be casualties when you try this fundamental pruning, especially if the shrubs are excessively old, but since you have nothing to lose, hack away and if some of them do die, simply replace them.

SEEK OUT SUCKERS

Frequently, an original shrub may be too old to be worth saving but may have produced a healthy crop of suckers — new shoots that emerge from the root system. These can be used to make useful replacement plants. When I took over an old farmhouse some years ago, the roadside boundary was marked by a vast hedge of white lilacs. Having been neglected for many years, it had grown to 3m/10ft or more and was now collapsing. Sections were dying of old age. I

ABOVE *Fast-growing plants — the evergreen shrub* Elaeagnus × ebbingei, *the deeply lobed, rampant perennial* Macleaya cordata *and the vigorous rose 'Wedding Day' — have all been put to good use turning an untidy old building into an ornamental garden feature.*

removed all the ancient wood, cutting the whole forest to ground level, but within a season, masses of suckers had sprung up and soon grew into a vigorous, renewed hedge.

▶ Where an ancient shrub has sent up lots of suckers, cut out all the old wood and allow selected suckers to grow into a replacement bush.

▶ Tease out suckers with some root attached and use these to make new plants as replacements or to fill gaps elsewhere.

SHORT-TERM PLANTS

While your butchered shrubs and lopped trees recover, be prepared to interplant them with temporary plants or with planted containers.

▶ Plant speedy trees and shrubs such as eucalyptus and abutilon to distract attention from severely pruned trees while they recover.

▶ Use rapid-growing perennials such as *Campanula lactiflora* or perennial asters in between cut-back shrubs until they spread again. A drift of foxgloves, planted between shorn shrubs, will provide quick height and colour, and will seed themselves and flower year after year; they will look as lovely when they play second fiddle to the re-grown shrubs as they did when they were the star attraction.

CUNNING CAMOUFLAGE

What at first might seem to be an eyesore can sometimes make the basis for an attractive feature. An old, dead stump, an ugly or misshapen tree, even a pile of stones may not be very pretty but might be useful as a vehicle for a rapid climber. The faster clematis species, for example, make short work of covering the biggest tree stumps. If the climbers become too untidy, all you need do is pull out unwanted material by the yard and snip it off.

▶ For rapid covering of a tall, unsightly object grow *Clematis montana*, which will scramble to over 6m/18ft in a couple of seasons and will be smothered with pink or white blossoms every spring.

The roots of old trees often spoil the surfaces of nearby pathways. As long as the standing capacity of the tree itself is not weakened, it is sometimes possible to cut out the offending part of the roots and repair the path, building a low wall along its edge to retain the tree's roots. If in doubt, consult a tree surgeon.

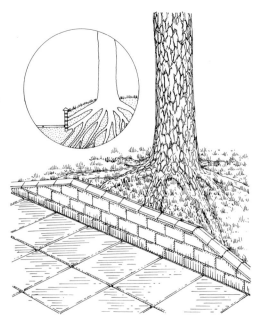

▶Liven up a dull evergreen tree by growing oriental species such as *Clematis serratifolia* or *C. tangutica* up into it. Their yellow, parchment-like flowers and fine, feathery seed heads, make a display from midsummer to early winter.

▶If you want to replace a dead tree, instead of removing it immediately, send a quick climber up it for instant luxuriant cover. Plant a replacement tree nearby and when this is large enough, chop down the old stump.

RECTIFY MISTAKES

There is a tendency to assume that once a plant is in place, it should not be disturbed. Such inflexibility is unnecessary, however. There is never any need to regard a planting, even of a substantial tree, as final and irrevocable. Mistakes are easy to rectify and plantings, even of trees and sizeable shrubs, can be temporary or medium term. Never fight shy of removing altogether trees that are in the wrong place. Even if they are in the prime of life, misplaced trees can spell ruin for your garden design.

▶If you make a mistake in positioning you can move most plants, as long as they are small enough to be manhandled and provided you do it during the dormant period between late autumn and early spring. Aftercare must be meticulous.

▶Water newly moved plants frequently and thoroughly to get the best out of them quickly; stake trees securely to prevent the wind from rocking them loose.

▶Before repositioning a tree or shrub, place a planted container where it is to go and leave it there for a while to see whether you like the new position. Pushing a series of cut branches into the ground or even standing members of the family, with their arms outstretched, on the chosen spots will also give you an idea.

ABOVE *An established rock garden has been revitalized by the addition of new plants, including* Sedum acre, Geranium dalmaticum *and, at the base,* Sisyrinchium striatum. *Older rock plants have been cut back to make them regenerate.*

OPPOSITE TOP *A luxuriant, productive mantle of runner beans camouflages a gnarled tree trunk for the summer. Trees are usually overlooked as potential supports for colourful fast climbers which can be encouraged to scramble up them in no time at all.*

RESTORING A GARDEN

Overgrown climbing plants should be cut right back and all their old wood taken out. They will respond by sending out pliable new growths which can be trained onto walls and fences. Shrubs, even if they have collapsed under their own weight, can be pruned hard to encourage vigorous regeneration from the base. Suckering shrubs can become new bushes if you lift and transplant their suckers.

Tired borders need digging over and their soil enriching with compost and some form of fertilizer in preparation for replanting. Complement existing plants with new ones to pack the borders and make the garden look long established.

Eyesores must be assessed and either eliminated or pressed into useful service. An ugly washing-line post, for instance, can be planted with climbers and thus given a new lease of life as an elegant pillar.

A good start is simply to clear away any rubbish – hard material and plant debris – and to take a good look at what is left. Broken down walls and fencing must be repaired or replaced, to reinforce the perimeter and provide a framework within which to work.

Existing pathways might be sound enough to need no more than patching up. Their edges can be planted up so that flowers spill over onto them. An overgrown lawn may need to be hacked back by hand at first, but will soon respond to feeding and regular trimming. Patches can be repaired with seed. Alternatively the whole lawn can be dug over and either sown or turfed.

An old tree can be retained as a central feature. The main branches will benefit from being thinned out to create a more open structure. Crossing, weak or contorted limbs should also be cut out. Water shoots – thin upright stems that grow along the main branches – need to be trimmed off. A very old, leaning tree may need propping.

A ruinous garden may have more potential than at first appears. Many of the original features often can be retained, restored to their former elegance and, in some cases, even improved. Take the garden section by section, getting one part squared away before moving on to the next.

Any leftover rocks or rubble can be piled up to make a feature over which climbers such as *Clematis alpina* can be encouraged to scramble. Alternatively, they could be used for building a rock garden which, once perennial weeds have been eliminated, could be planted with alpines.

CREATING A MICROCLIMATE

PLUG WINDY GAPS
Build on existing forms of shelter

PERMEABLE WINDBREAKS
Slow wind down

TRAP THE SUN
Create a warm spot

PROVIDE SHADE
Climbers for filtering sunlight

PROTECTIVE PLANTING
Place tender plants windward of evergreens

OPPOSITE *A small, crammed town garden has been made even more sheltered by planting trees on its boundary and furnishing its walls with thick growths of climbing plants.*

To develop at top speed, plants need to be in rude health as well as happy in their environment. But many of the plants that we grow in our gardens are exotic species and are somewhat out of their element. Few would survive, unaided, in the wild and even those that are truly hardy perform all the better for a little care and management. Artificial hybrids of garden plants are even more dependent on good management and so a well-planted garden is, in effect, an artificial habitat. Anyone aspiring to a decent garden, therefore, must ensure a favourable environment within the plot. Even better would be an area where weather conditions are actually modified to the advantage of the plants, that is, a microclimate.

Creating a microclimate is itself a short-cut strategy – the more favourable the conditions are, the faster the plants will grow. In any garden, the main limiting factor, apart from soil, is climate. Winter temperatures decide which plants survive and which need protection. Summer heatwaves, wind, snow or freezing winters all help to determine which plants perform best in your area.

Rainfall is crucial, not just how much, but how well distributed it is through the season. Successful gardeners learn, not just how to work within the limitations of climate, but also how to steal a trick from whatever the weather throws at them.

The first and most important move to improve any garden is to give it shelter. As soon as the wind has been reduced, the climate within the boundaries will improve and the plants benefit. Even a relatively quiet garden suffers when the wind gets up and few gardens are quiet. Neighbouring buildings and trees may provide shelter, especially if they are sited to block prevailing winds.

Buildings and walls can make things worse, though. Air currents squeeze between them and are accelerated, sometimes to destructive speeds. Walls, rather than preventing wind, cause damaging eddy currents when it swirls round them or over their tops. The most effective windbreaks, therefore, are those that slow the air down but permit it to pass through.

▶**Take full advantage of any existing features which might help give protection against prevailing wind – street trees, neighbouring garages or houses and high boundary fences can all be a blessing here. Plug potentially dangerous gaps in walls or between buildings with a screen or strategic planting of shrubs or trees to either stop or slow the wind.**

A rough and ready screen can be grown very quickly using high speed shrubs such as buddleia, willow, rubus, rampant shrub roses and laurel (left to right), and even bramble species. They will look somewhat gappy in their first year (top) but towards the end of their second year they will have closed ranks to make an effective and colourful hedge (bottom).

After a few seasons these shrubs can be cut almost to ground level to form a thicket of young growths. Later still, when other, more select sheltering plants have grown up, parts or all of the high-speed hedge can be removed.

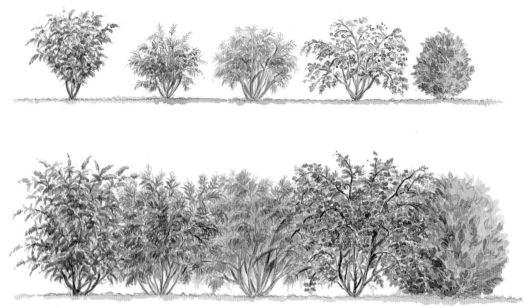

RIGHT *A well-sheltered city garden sports tropical and exotic-looking foliage planted densely for maximum impact. Protected from harsh conditions, most of the plants will grow large in a single season.*

▶ Woven screens and trellises make effective windbreaks and have the advantage of being easy and quick to install.

▶ Living material, either in the form of hedges or as informal plantings of trees and shrubs are even more effective.

One of the secondary benefits of erecting or growing windbreaks is that they often help to trap the sun. In cold areas, this can be almost as important as protection from the wind. If the sun trap becomes too hot, it may need to be shaded in places.

▶ Shade a sun trap with quick-growing vines or other deciduous climbers on a framework; in winter precious daylight will get through.

▶ Even on the shady side of a shelter, the environment is improved. Apart from providing planting opportunities for shade lovers, it also reduces the ambient temperature and so the rate at which the soil dries out. That, too, increases the range of plants which can be grown.

As soon as the first shelters are in position, the plants begin to grow quickly and provide secondary shelter for each other. The bigger they get, the more shelter they provide. And once the tougher species have got themselves well established, more delicate plants can be introduced.

▶ In cold areas, flank tender shrubs with evergreens to give them a better chance of surviving harsh winters.

THE GOOD SOIL

Soil is a mixture of minerals, air, water, dissolved mineral salts, dead organic material and billions of living organisms. Plant roots have evolved, not just as anchors but to absorb food from the soil's resources. Water is necessary to operate a plant's life support system, and minerals, absorbed along with the water, are essential nutrients. Some plants have a special relationship with soil micro-organisms and languish without healthy populations of them among their roots.

The optimum soil is light and easy to work, with a tendency to crumble rather than break into clods or collapse into powder. It is rich in organic matter, free draining and yet moisture retentive during dry periods. An experienced gardener can tell, by feel, just what sort of condition the soil is in but, if you are not sure just how good yours is, look at your plants.

The physical condition of the soil is known as structure. When the soil has a crumbly texture, with lots of air spaces in between the particles, water and air are present in the right mix. Roots will not penetrate saturated, compacted soil since they need air to develop healthily.

Organic content, mostly consisting of dead vegetation in various stages of decay, is important for helping to preserve a good structure and for the general well-being of plants. It is transported to different levels by earthworms — your most valuable full-time gardeners!

Plants manufacture food from carbon dioxide in the air, but they also need essential minerals such as nitrogen, phosphorus and potassium as well as smaller quantities of a whole range of chemical elements which include copper, iron, manganese and so on, all derived from the soil. In an artificial situation

IMPROVE SOIL STRUCTURE
Dig deep, adding manure or compost

AVOID COMPACTION
Try to keep off the soil

RETAIN MOISTURE
Mulch generously to save on watering

ABOVE *Stepping stones mark out a path through a vegetable patch, minimizing pressure on the soil and thus avoiding compaction as the garden is tended.*

OPPOSITE By maintaining fertility and keeping organic content high with regular additions of compost, a flower border can be kept in tip-top condition and looking good through most of the year as it sports a succession of plants.

like a garden, the soil's fertility needs to be maintained by applying fertilizer on a regular basis. Both farmyard manure and artificial plant foods provide these minerals and, as plant material rots down, it also releases nutrients back into the soil.

Drainage is essential for successful plant growth. If soil is not adequately drained it becomes waterlogged and plants will not grow in it. Furthermore, poorly drained soil tends to lose its structure and, in summer, can dry to a hard, cracked condition causing plants that formerly suffered from a surfeit of water at the roots to die of drought. Plants that struggle to grow in wet soil fail to develop large, questing root systems and so are far more susceptible to drought stress than those growing in free-draining conditions.

SOIL CARE

It is crucial, therefore, to keep your soil in the best condition to guarantee a quickly developing garden.

Old-fashioned double digging may seem an odd route to take for a short cut but it could save a great deal of time later on, especially if the soil you have inherited is in poor condition. Double digging is laborious to be sure, but, having dug through once, you should not have to repeat the

chore for many years. Your efforts, in either a brand new or a tired garden, will pay dividends by getting the plants off to a flying start.

▶ **A thorough working through, digging up to 30cm/12in in poor soil, breaking up compacted lumps and incorporating compost or manure as you go, will help to bring tired soil to life. Thus, what seems a long job is, in fact, a short cut. The poorer the soil, the more treatment it will need but even the most ideal soils are all the better for being looked after.**

▶ **Heavy clay soils benefit from the addition of pea shingle, grit, leaf mould or even ashes to break up the raw clods. The simplest way to incorporate these materials is to spread them evenly over the surface before you start digging.**

Treat your borders with great respect, especially when they have been deeply dug. Walking on soil, running vehicles over it or allowing children to play on it results in compaction: all the air is squeezed out and, on heavy soils, the ground can set almost like concrete. In wet weather keep off it altogether, or lay planks for walking on to distribute pressure over a wider area of the soil surface.

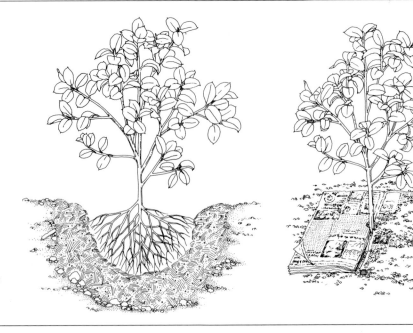

When planting out new shrubs it is important to get them off to a good start. Make the planting hole larger than is needed to accommodate the roots and incorporate a generous amount of soil-improving compost mixed with a slow-release fertilizer. For further protection, you can place a mulching layer of several sheets of newspaper, with a slit made for the stem, just under the last portion of the soil backfill. This will reduce the rate of water loss from the ground during dry weather but it may also inhibit artificial watering. When watering the plant, therefore, be sure to soak the ground around it thoroughly.

▶Make sure the design of your garden allows you to tend to borders and other exposed soil areas without having to step onto the soil. If you have to walk on soil, limit the number of times you do, even when it is apparently dry.

▶Remedy areas of compacted ground. Either dig the affected ground or simply push the tines of a large garden fork in, at 15cm/6in intervals, as far as they will go and ease the haft back and forth to crack and break up the crust.

▶Summer drought can stop plants in their tracks unless the soil is protected from the worst of the dry weather. Spread mulches of chopped bark, compost or leaf mould (approximately 7.5cm/3in thick) over the surface between the plants, to minimize moisture loss during dry summers.

FEEDING PLANTS

Slow-release fertilizers, such as bonemeal, or specially formulated products, are invaluable because they make regular feeding through the season unnecessary and so cut down on chore time later on. But, with annuals and the more gross-feeding perennials, slow-release products can run out before the end of the growing season. Pale foliage and a slowing down of growth are early symptoms which should be treated right away.

▶Get shrubs off to a good start and then sustain rapid growth by incorporating an application of slow-release fertilizer into the soil when you plant them.

▶Keep a regular look-out for tell-tale signs of 'plant hunger'. Restore health and growth rate quickly with foliar feeds – liquid fertilizer sprayed onto foliage – but, beware of over-feeding. Too much nitrogen causes over-rapid, soft growth which is then susceptible to disease.

▶Annual bedding displays, especially in containers or hanging baskets, need a regular boost of fertilizer, in some cases as often as once a week, to keep them healthy and looking their best.

4

SHORT CUTS TO GARDEN BOUNDARIES

Although layout is important, the essence of a good garden is structure. And the first and most telling features in any garden – those which best create the feeling of maturity and establishment – are such solid, three dimensional structures as wall, fences, hedges, pergolas and arches. Thus, if lead time needs to be minimized on any garden project, the boundaries are an important element where effective change can be brought about very quickly, sometimes instantly.

From the short-cut gardener's point of view, some aspects of these structural features are more satisfactory than others. The following pages discuss how boundary structures can influence a garden and how existing ones can be enhanced to create an all-important established feel in the minimum of time.

Extra height has been given to this well-covered wall by standing large pots along the top. Walls provide shelter but, to create a mature-looking feature, they need to be furnished with plants.

PERIMETERS AND PARTITIONS

CAPITALIZE ON BOUNDARIES
Include perimeters in your design

PLANT UP PERIMETERS
Breathe life into walls and fences

INVOLVE BUILDINGS
Extend planting surfaces

INTERNAL PARTITIONS
Make 'rooms' or screen off areas

HARMONIZE MATERIALS
Choose the right type of boundary

All properties need to have their perimeters marked in some way. But boundary structures do a lot more for gardens than merely mark out their dimensions. Fences, walls, screens and hedges have a number of functions. They are useful for privacy. They may need to be pet or child proof, keeping puppies or toddlers safely away from the dangerous road outside. They may act as screens, keeping out the wind, trapping the sun or providing refreshing shade. They can even be surprisingly effective at reducing traffic noise.

Although they are primarily functional, boundaries should be included in a garden's design and contribute to its overall beauty. Bare fences or unsympathetic walls make even the most established garden look naked and unwelcoming. But as prominent features, taller than much of what surrounds them, they should be made as interesting as possible to enhance the rest of the design. Far from presenting a problem, this can simply be part of the overall planting strategy, and often turns out to be the biggest single short cut to maturity.

Where a building constitutes a garden boundary, its potential should not be overlooked. The walls of a house, garage or any other outbuilding can be furnished with plants so that what may look like a barren habitat can be made green and living.

If you do not have any boundary structures, or do not like the ones you do have, you can, of course, build new ones to suit your taste and pocket. Fortunately, the most expensive are not always the most effective.

INTERNAL BOUNDARIES

Apart from the essential perimeter boundary structures, you may wish to erect partitions and screens within the garden itself. Small areas can often be improved by adding screens or plant-

ing hedges. If you grow vegetables, for instance, or want to create a play area, install a plunge pool, or keep poultry, you will probably want to screen these special areas from the rest of the garden. Even within a purely ornamental garden, dividing off areas adds that element of mystery and surprise which can be so delightful. Indeed, one of the features of the typical British country garden is that it is divided into 'rooms' – relatively small enclosures, each with its special mood and style.

Where vistas are planned, the narrow views are usually bordered by screens or rows of trees. In an open garden, where wide views are important, screens can be used to create pockets of protection for special plantings, or to disguise parts of the area so that they can only be seen from different angles.

So, whatever your gardening style, it is a safe bet that your design will include a number of boundaries, screens, fences or hedges.

For guidance, each garden element is given a short-cut rating to demonstrate just how effective it is likely to be. The rating is necessarily generalized because what works well as a short-cut strategy in one garden may not produce such good results in another.

★★★ Extra quick. Looks finished and mature within a single growing season or even sooner

★★ Quick. Bears some results in the first season and has reached a degree of maturity by the second

★ Moderately fast. Looks good in its second or third season

ABOVE *Stark new fencing, even with elegant posts, is improved when furnished with living plants. Sweet peas, simple to grow and manage, will create a large and fragrant display in a single summer and will also provide a succession of cut flowers to take indoors.*

LEFT *Covered with the climbing rose 'Kathleen Harrop', which provides colour all summer, the author's house wall makes a fine garden backdrop. The pink* Centranthus ruber *in the foreground is an early highlight that can be cut back to flower again in autumn.*

OPPOSITE *Raised beds at the foot of a wall provide extra planting opportunities for climbers, especially where the wall footing is set into a concrete foundation. Forming a niche for a statue and by encouraging vigorous growth of the wall plants, these beds have turned a boundary into a feature.*

WALLS, FENCING AND TRELLIS

DISGUISE AN UGLY WALL
Improve its appearance

FAST FENCING
Make an instant boundary

ADD APPEAL
Incorporate peepholes in
boundaries

TRY TRELLIS
A quick solution to many
problems

CREATE AN ILLUSION
Play with trellis shapes

It is difficult to evaluate man-made boundaries in isolation. We need to think of them as vehicles for plants because so few look their best until they are furnished with living material.

WALLS ★

Walls can be beautiful. Although not a short-cut strategy in themselves, as design and planting devices they are invaluable assets worth implementing because of their long-term effects. Furnished with a good selection of climbing plants, any wall can become a wonderful feature that will outlast pretty well everything else.

Where no wall exists you can always build one, but they are among the most costly of structures and need much skill in the building. Materials need to be chosen with care and in sympathy with neighbouring buildings. A nineteenth-century brick cottage would not look comfortable with a concrete block wall running up to it, just as a modern, glass-clad

structure would look ludicrous set in the midst of ancient limestone walling.

Old stone ★★
A wall built with old or mellow stone looks a dream and imparts instant maturity, but will cost a small fortune.

Old brick ★★
You can achieve instant maturity by building a new wall using old, weathered bricks but to look good they must be in keeping with nearby buildings.

New brick ★
New brick is cheaper, obviously, than old, but takes longer to get that weathered look.

Building block ★
Composition building blocks can have their appearance 'improved'. You can paint them, texture them, render them with plaster, or even clad one side with something else. Stone cladding would give a traditional feel, but you could experiment with other materials.

PILLARS ★

A happy compromise between cost and effectiveness is to erect brick or stone pillars and fix wooden panels or trellis in between. This can look surprisingly good and innumerable styles can be designed to incorporate other structures such as pergolas, bowers or gazebos.

FENCING ★★

A wooden fence brings about an instant transformation to a garden boundary. Versatile and useful as it is, though, timber will rot at some point and need replacing. Even hardwoods rot eventually, but the life of all timber can be lengthened with a wood preservative.

Good fencing can be as cheap and easy to install as a row of posts with thin wooden slats nailed to them, or as expensive as solid oak posts and panels.

Woven panels ★★
Woven timber strip panels are cheap, popular and effective, provided they are anchored to really sturdy, preferably hardwood, posts, but the panels themselves are seldom strong enough to carry much weight.

A plain or new garden wall can be made attractive and mature looking quickly. Placing containers along the top of a wall creates interest and adds height. Pots or troughs planted with ivy leaf pelargoniums or trailing nasturtiums would make a fine summer show; in winter these could be replaced with ivy and wallflowers. If the ground is paved over, preventing direct planting, containers can be placed against the wall and furnished with decorative subjects such as abutilons or, for a combination of use and ornament, with tomatoes or even small fruit trees.

ABOVE *A tiny opening through an old stone wall allows an inviting glimpse of a sheltered garden beyond. New walls can be constructed incorporating such a feature, or one could be cut into an existing structure.*

OPPOSITE *These elegant pillars, topped with ivy-clad balls, have been built with second-hand bricks. They would have made a strong feature on their own but, planted as they are with climbers, they form a perfect backdrop to the garden.*

*OPPOSITE TOP Rustic trellis,
especially when adorned with fast-
growing roses, can look established
very quickly. In favourable
conditions, it can become covered
with flowers and greenery in its
first season.*

*OPPOSITE BOTTOM LEFT Trellis has
been used on a grand scale to
create a 'room', providing the
opportunity to establish an area
with a different character within a
larger garden.*

▶When installing woven panel fencing, suspend a practicable system of wires between the posts on to which to tie climbing plants. Climbing vegetation can be very heavy, especially when wet, and can damage the weave of panels if fixed directly to it.

Hardwood ★

Hardwood fencing is more expensive, but it lasts longer and is usually sturdy enough to carry the weight of, say, a large, overgrown, wet clematis. When selecting hardwood do spare a thought for its provenance and ensure that it comes from a replenishable source.

PEEPHOLES

A solid boundary that can be seen through in places, offers a tempting view of delights on the other side. Windows, arches and even gateways through boundaries can be structured to allow enticing views through them. Humans are inquisitive creatures and cannot resist peeping. I remember reading about a Japanese garden designer who enclosed an entire garden, which was set by the sea, with screens and hedges completely shutting out the elements beyond. But at the precise point where guests bent to wash before the tea ceremony, a small chink treated them to a surprise view of the sea breaking on the shore.

▶A completely circular 'moon' gate makes a surprising feature with a touch of the Chinoiserie about it.

▶Add a charming extra dimension to a solid wall or fence by cutting a peephole through it – no more than 60cm/2ft long and 45cm/18in high, protected perhaps by a decorative wrought or cast iron grille – to offer a delightfully tempting glimpse of what is on the other side.

TRELLIS ★★★

Trellis is the short-cut gardener's greatest friend. It is easy to erect, can be fairly durable, has potential for elegance but, above all, it looks 'gardenish' as soon as it has been put up. And because it is so lightweight in its structure – even when constructed of heavy duty timber – it allows small quantities of plant material to go a long way. Its versatility allows it to be used in a number of ways.

The only disadvantage of trellis is that it does not usually last as long as fencing. But that is a small price to pay for a material with such a multitude of uses.

Wooden slats have been fixed to make lines and angles which give the impression of a niche when, in fact, the whole assembly is on a flat wall. Trellis can be great for visual cheating. Besides being an amusing trick, the trompe l'oeil can be used to give the impression of more space. For instance, it can suggest a non-existent exit or even a large garden area beyond a screen.

▶ Use trellis anywhere in the garden, either freestanding or fixed to a wall, to make an instant, permanent boundary feature.

▶ Erect temporary trellis screens to disguise areas while they are developing or not ready to show off. Plant it up with quick climbers until the area beyond has matured and is ready to be included in the garden scheme. When the time comes to remove the screen, you can use it somewhere else.

▶ Create innumerable, and surprisingly effective, designs by joining trellis to other structures such as pergolas, bowers or gazebos.

▶ Fix trellis to an ugly wall as anchorage for rampant climbers so that they can shoot up to hide the surface beneath.

▶ Alter the apparent shape and outline of buildings using trellis. You can connect one to the other, for example, or disguise or even re-shape ugly corners.

▶ From a practical point of view, trellis is surprisingly effective as a windbreak.

Standing trellis may look bare in its first year, even after climbing plants have been introduced. Hanging baskets or pots fixed to the trellis will provide colour while the climbers become established. Even after the climbers have developed, a scattering of suspended containers can continue to add highlights to the display. For an informal effect leave trellis in natural wood; paint it white or dark green to achieve a more traditional flavour for use in a formal garden.

FURNISHING BOUNDARIES

RIGHT *A boundary wall has been turned into a central feature. Containers placed at its foot and arches set with such vigorous climbers as golden hop all help to achieve a quick maturity. Roses and honeysuckles contribute fragrance.*

OPPOSITE BOTTOM *Festooned for the summer with fragrant sweet peas and scarlet runner beans, trellis has been used to turn an otherwise exposed spot into a private corner.*

RAPID CLIMBERS
For the fastest cover

FIXING POINTS
Provide wires or hooks for tying plants to

TIE IN REGULARLY
Keep loose ends tidy

FRAGRANCE
Choose sweet-smelling climbers

An unclothed boundary, whether perimeter or internal, imparts its nakedness to other parts of the garden, lending an unfinished feel to the whole. The idea is to furnish it with a living mantle that complements the rest of the planting. But how can you create a large screen that looks mature within a single growing season? The answer is with cunning use of fast-growing climbers which, if properly trained, will rampage over man-made boundaries and supports, breathing life into them.

▶ Equip any structure you want plants to grow up with anchoring screws or vine eyes and wires to ensure secure support. At first, be ready to tie in loose ends on an almost daily basis. Later, many of the plants will cling to themselves, making a thick mat of foliage, stems and flowers.

HERBACEOUS CLIMBERS ★★★

Annual herbaceous climbers, especially, can be surprisingly rapid. In warm summers and in a well-prepared, fertile soil, they will put on metres of growth, covering their supports with greenery at first, and then make a climax with flowers.

▶ Raise *Cobaea scandens*, technically a perennial but fast enough to be grown as an annual in cold countries, under glass in spring and plant it out after the risk of frost has passed. It has evergreen foliage, large, bell-shaped flowers and then, as a bonus, enchanting seed heads to provide interest throughout the changing seasons. *Eccremocarpus scaber* is equally rapid and grows even more easily from seed.

Extremely fast climbers can disguise an ugly wall in the minimum of time. *Cobaea scandens* (left) contributes soft purple, blue or white flowers and, later on, seed heads. The kiwi fruit (*Actinidia chinensis*) (centre left) is fully hardy but will only fruit in warm conditions and if male and female plants are together. The herbaceous golden hop (*Humulus lupulus* 'Aurea') (centre right) needs cutting to the ground each winter. Large-leaved *Vitis coignetiae* (right) colours well in autumn. Alternative climbers include *Eccremocarpus scaber*, jasmine, *Clematis armandii* or any of the climbing honeysuckles.

▶Grow sweet peas for their evocative fragrance, even though they are not such rapid coverers as some other plants.

OTHER CLIMBERS ★★

With such a wide choice of climbing and wall plants in cultivation, you can be sure to find plenty that will thrive in whatever conditions prevail in your garden. By far the most effective for this job are clematis and honeysuckles.

▶When making your selection of climbers, check the habit carefully. The fastest growing are not always the best choice for every situation. Some may be too invasive for a small site, or may not offer enough in the way of flowers. Certain plants, particularly Russian bindweed (*Polygonum baldschuanicum*), *Akebia quinata* and certain clematis species, may be too vigorous and prove hard to remove once planted.

▶To accelerate a sense of height, try creating screens from containers planted with quick growers. Large pots, with trellis fixed above them for support, can accommodate a mix of annual climbers, such as sweet peas or nasturtiums and more permanent honeysuckles or summer jasmine. The resulting screens will give you something to enjoy immediately while the rest of the planting develops.

HEDGES

TOP SPEED HEDGING PLANTS

Evergreen

Aucuba japonica ★
Elaeagnus × ebbingei ★★★
Elaeagnus pungens
    'Maculata' ★
Griselinia littoralis ★★
Picea abies (Christmas
    tree) ★
Prunus laurocerasus
    'Zabelliana' ★★
× Cupressocyparis
    leylandii ★★★

Deciduous

Carpinus betula
    (Hornbeam) ★★
Cornus mas ★
Cornus mas 'Variegata' ★
Prunus cerasifera
    'Pissardii' ★★

Good for flowers

Escallonia macrantha ★★
Forsythia 'Lynwood' ★★
Olearia haastii ★
Osmanthus × burkwoodii ★
Ribes sanguineum
    (Flowering currant) ★★★

Best for informal hedges

Berberis darwinii ★★
Crataegus monogyna
    (Hawthorn) ★★
Prunus lusitanica ★
Rosa species ★★★
Tamarix pentandra ★★

Best for close clipping

Lonicera nitida ★★
Ligustrum ovalifolium ★★
Ligustrum japonicum ★
Cupressus macrocarpa ★★★

Plants for tapestry hedges

Acer campestre ★★
Philadelphus coronarius
    'Aureus' ★
Prunus spinosa ★
Elaeagnus × ebbingei ★★★
Pyracantha – all ★★
Viburnum lantana ★★
Viburnum opulus ★★

In the short-cut garden, a hedge is a useful device, not necessarily the fastest to mature but certainly one of the most mature looking once it is established. As well as being useful for boundaries or barriers, hedges can be made into interesting features themselves: they can act as rear curtains to colourful borders; they can be clipped into fanciful shapes; kept trimmed to less than a metre high even though they may have reached a great age; or they can be allowed to grow to amazing heights.

The quickest hedge will only develop at top speed if conditions are ideal. If your soil has good natural fertility, some of the following recommendations may seem to be a little excessive. But on poor soil it will be even more important to get the hedge off to a good a start as soon as possible. Planting a hedge with care may seem unnecessarily arduous but the payoff is accelerated development and therefore earlier maturity.

▶ **To give a hedge a head start, first dig a single trench, deeper and wider than the roots if possible. Replace some of the soil with a mix of leaf mould or well rotted manure and any other mulching material, mixing well. Space the plants evenly and add bonemeal, or another slow-release fertilizer, and tread them firmly in. In exposed positions, stake securely to minimize wind rock.**

►Prune a newly planted, non-coniferous hedge back by at least one third to stimulate thicker growth and ensure that the hedge will be as dense at its bottom as at the top. (Coniferous plants, which are unable to regenerate from brown wood, should never be cut hard back in this way; they do not need trimming until they have reached their desired height.)

►Aftercare is important during a hedge's first season. Water it regularly to help to sustain growth. Trim lightly half way through the growing season and check regularly to see that wind rock is not a problem. One or two plants may die in the early stages; replace these the following autumn. Do not be alarmed at the size difference. Your replacements will soon catch up!

Unlike walls, even the fastest hedges take a while to establish. But they must be allowed to grow unencumbered, so any temporary, short-cut screen or barrier will need to be placed far enough away to avoid inhibiting their growth.

►Encourage rapid growth of a new hedge by placing a temporary screen windward of it.

Making the right choice of hedging plant needs care. There are so many factors to consider. Will it be evergreen? What height do you want your hedge to grow to? Will it be strictly formal and severely clipped, or do you want a rougher, less formal screen? How often are you prepared to clip − once a season or once a month? The problem is, the more you look into the whole business of hedges, the more spoilt you are for choice!

There are flowering hedges like *Ribes sanguineum*, evergreen hedges like holly or yew and deciduous hedges, like beech and hornbeam. Beech and hornbeam keep their clothing of dead leaves through the winter months, making them as effective as evergreens but with more profound changes in colour through the seasons.

Some of the most unlikely plants, from asparagus fern or sugar cane in warm climates to Christmas trees in the cold north, have been trained into hedges.

Some hedging plants, such as yew, holly (all

A trellis can form an instant screen but, positioned 45cm/18in away from a newly planted hedge, it will afford protection while the hedge develops as well as acting as a barrier. Later, when the hedge has matured, the trellis can be removed.

An unsightly concrete block wall can be completely hidden behind a screen of quick-growing ivy, clipped evenly to give the impression of a high, formal hedge.

Ilex aquifolium and *I. altaclarensis* cultivars), although slow, are worth considering for inclusion in a short-cut garden because of their great long-term value. They may be needed to take over later, when temporary strategies have gone beyond maturity into senescence.

►Before selecting your hedging plants do some research − there are many speedy hedging plants but they do all have special qualities, and, inevitably, their own special disadvantages too.

Many of the hedging plants described on page 123 are suitable for both informal and formal use. Many of these reach mature size quickly to make enchanting informal screens.

OPPOSITE *A beech hedge, which retains its leaves during winter, is fronted by hydrangeas, sarcococca and variegated box to create an informal screen. Hellebore foliage adds to the evergreen content and, later, will provide flowers at the foot of the hedge.*

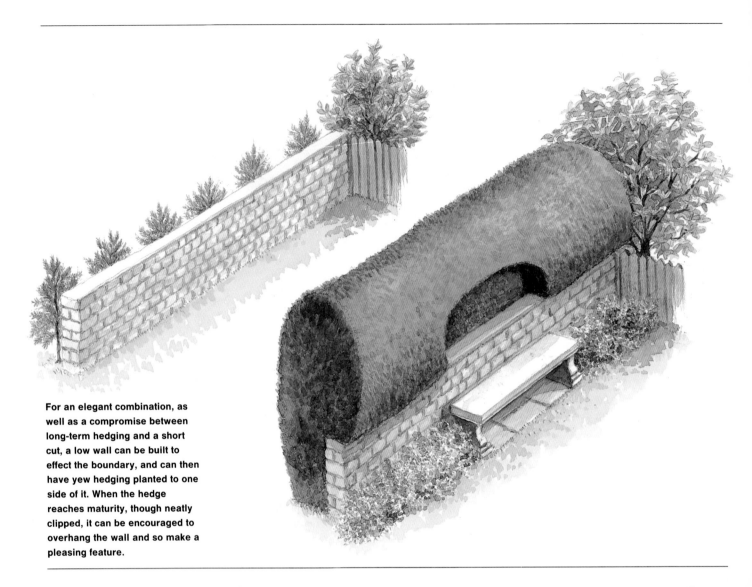

For an elegant combination, as well as a compromise between long-term hedging and a short cut, a low wall can be built to effect the boundary, and can then have yew hedging planted to one side of it. When the hedge reaches maturity, though neatly clipped, it can be encouraged to overhang the wall and so make a pleasing feature.

OPPOSITE TOP LEFT *Tree mallows grow fast to make a colourful summer screen but need to be cut back each spring to ensure vigorous growth.*

OPPOSITE BOTTOM *A tapestry hedge of alternating golden and green privet plants has been cut in an undulating pattern which reflects the patchwork landscape in the background.*

▶Most vigorous flowering shrubs grow well as hedging but the more severely clipped they are, the less readily they flower. The best form of compromise for a flowering hedge is to give it an annual trim immediately after flowering, but to be tolerant of a certain amount of straggliness, especially in the first few seasons.

TAPESTRY

A tapestry hedge can be a delightful feature in an informal garden. It is simply a collection of hedging plants, all with contrasting characteristics. Some flower, some bear colourful autumn berries and others may be evergreen so that the hedge's winter appearance remains lively and interesting. You can make up almost any combination you like but make sure the plants you choose all have similar growth rates so that

weaker ones are not crowded out by bullies. At first, the fledgling tapestry hedge will probably look a mess but, as it matures and its shape develops, the patches or blocks of different colours and textures will become more obvious. I dislike formally alternated plants say, blue-green and golden conifers, because the results, to me, look rather unnatural – but that is merely a matter of personal taste and opinion.

There is an almost infinite number of combination possibilities in a tapestry hedge and insufficient space here to provide detailed recipes. Some of the most useful hedging plants for a tapestry hedge are listed on page 60.

▶For a really fast, colourful hedge, plant a mixture of different shrub roses. Lilac is also very fast growing and, if several varieties are used, makes an attractive display in late spring.

Leyland cypress makes a fine hedge within three or four years. Whilst growing to the desired height, the feathery green foliage must not be cut. But once the trees have reached the correct height, they should be clipped once a year in a wedge shape with a flat top.

▶A likely mix for a tapestry hedge could include holly, whose bottle-green winter foliage makes a lovely contrast with the tan of dead beech leaves. Those two plants alone would make a bewitching combination but if you added *Cornus alba* 'Spaethii' for summer foliage and winter twigs; hazel for winter catkins and perhaps a hawthorn or two for wildlife accommodation, your hedge would have constant interest.

▶Other combinations for short-cut tapestry hedges could include *Cotoneaster lacteus*, for red berries, planted with golden privet for foliage colour.

WILDLIFE-FRIENDLY HEDGES

Hedges are important for wildlife in that they provide shelter in winter, shade in summer and a food supply — not just in the more obvious form of berries for birds but also in the insects and other invertebrates they harbour. These form links in the food chain of a great many birds, small mammals, reptiles and amphibians.

The finest wildlife hedge I have seen was developed from an old field hedge and contained hawthorn, hazel, *Cornus sanguinea*, blackthorn, holly and beech. Ivy had been allowed to grow up into it, and flowered at its crown. It was — and still is for all I know — trimmed, once a year in late winter, before the birds started nesting.

5

SHORT CUTS TO THE GARDEN OUTLINE

The backbone of any well-designed, well-planted garden is its outline. Outline provides the necessary shape, skeleton or three dimensional profile on which the rest of the planting and design hangs. Height is crucial in outline planning because the overall design tends to work around the highest feature or plant. In a mature garden, much of the outline consists of living plants, in particular trees and shrubs, probably backed up with man-made structures and ornaments to complete the effect.

In the short-cut garden, as well as long-term outline, we need artificial aids for the early stages while we wait for the rest of the garden to mature. Here are some ways in which a good outline can be developed quickly.

Trellis, a large central urn and spaced, upright golden conifers help to make this light and airy garden enticing. Such features are invaluable tools for creating a pleasing garden profile.

MAN-MADE FEATURES

BUILD A PERGOLA
Improve the outline

ERECT PILLARS
Provide height for climbers

ELEGANT ARCHES
Transform entrances

PLANT UP STEPS
Turn changes in level into a
feature

OBJECTS OF INTEREST
Site sculpture and other items as
focal points

Artificially constructed outline features provide the empty structure into which plants can grow. They usually occupy key points and are thus conspicuous. In old gardens, such structures often nestle among mature shrubs and tall trees. In a new, short-cut garden, they tend to look a little stark and raw but, with cunning placement and clever planting, they can do a great deal to foster the impression of age and stature quickly.

Although such features may be purely decorative, some of the cleverest combine function with ornament. A new garden, especially, offers plenty of scope. Since you need something as utilitarian as a potting shed, for example, might it not be fun for it to double as a gazebo or a little folly? That way, you could turn a building of mundane use into an attractive feature and, instead of concealing it, site it at some central point in the garden.

PERGOLAS, POSTS AND PILLARS

One of the quickest and easiest ways of raising the profile in a new garden is to build a pergola and smother it with fast-growing climbing plants. Depending on the degree of their complexity, they are fairly easily and swiftly erected, and will immediately transform the outline of any garden.

The most basic designs consist of little more than upright timber poles with crosspieces in between. The next step in sophistication is a double row of uprights with crosspieces across the top as well as along either side. But the ultimate pergola design is the classic form of a double line of brick or stone pillars with heavy timber crosspieces. Such a structure is so elegant in itself that it immediately contributes presence and maturity to a garden, even before plants have been trained up it.

An obelisk can be cheaply made out of inverted sections of fan-shaped trellis which can be left as natural wood or painted before being furnished with climbers. Plants of moderate vigour are best so that garlands drape themselves over the structure.

RIGHT *Four columns to create the effect of a classic temple, enhanced by stacked containers and a path paved with old stone, serve as a centrepiece to the planting of pansies and blue meconopsis in this formal layout.*

OPPOSITE *Given a man-made framework on which to grow, speedy climbing plants such as clematis and rambling roses provide the fastest and most natural-looking shelter.*

In the kitchen garden, a metal arch is as effective for growing climbing fruits such as loganberries or blackberries as it is for ornamental plants. Indeed, such fruits are, themselves, ornamental.

▶Pergolas are widely available in kit form at modest cost and are straight-foward to erect. Planted with copiously flowering and sweet-smelling climbing plants they cannot fail to bring about the instant transformation of even the humblest of gardens.

▶Besides being attractive vehicles for plants, pergolas make useful area dividers. Place one carefully and it can form an interesting backdrop when viewed at right angles but reveal a vista to anyone looking along it.

▶Before installing a pergola, make sure it is at least at least 2.3m/7ft above the ground, to allow sufficient clearance for anyone walking beneath, even when climbing plants have covered the pergola from one side to the other and their abundant blossoms are hanging low.

▶Wrought iron and mild steel are alternative materials with great potential for artistic pergolas, as well as for arches, tunnels or whatever else you can dream up in the way of novel climbing frames.

▶Individual timber posts and brick or stone pillars also make interesting features in themselves, whether standing isolated or in groups. They can be tall, so that the climbers trained up them tower above the surrounding plantings, or they may be no more than short posts, simply there to raise the heads of selected plants above the rest.

▶Additionally, posts and pillars can be linked together in various ways to bring these design features together. Large ropes, sagging like inverted arches between pillars and furnished with garlands of climbing roses, for instance, have been used to good effect in several famous gardens.

ARCHES

A garden entrance must be entrancing! To go through, to enter, is to take a step into a different place, perhaps into the unknown! From a design point of view, it is worth trying to

LEFT *This gateway has almost disappeared among rapid plants – not only climbing honeysuckle but also such herbaceous monsters as the giant thistle (*Onopordum arabicum*).*

OPPOSITE TOP *Rapidly climbing species such as* Parthenocissus quinquefolia *soon cover a metal frame. Autumn colour is superb with this plant but one has to remember that it has no leaves at all in winter.*

make every entrance either dramatic, inviting or mysterious. Whether Romanesque and rounded or Gothic and pointed, the arch is a beautiful shape, especially when clad with living plants. Even the simplest construction, whether over a gateway or freestanding and leading from one garden area to another, can support a fast-growing climber or rambler, laden all summer long with blossom.

▶ Make gateways grand simply by constructing arches over them. These can be made of solid wood so that they cannot be seen through until the gate is opened, or they can be fashioned in ironwork, providing a tempting window to what lies beyond.

▶ Plant up an arch with honeysuckle to provide welcoming fragrance. For year-round cover include an ivy, either green or variegated, which will soon create a luxuriant growth.

An arch over a gate is easy to furnish with rapid climbers or even lax shrubs such as *Lavatera thuringiaca* 'Barnsley', as shown here. If it becomes leggy or untidy it can be cut back.

▶Single arches are amusing to walk through but rows of arches — arranged side by side, like cloisters — can have a greater impact.

▶Arches arranged parallel with, but close to a boundary hedge or wall can create a trompe l'oeil, giving the impression that there is more garden on the other side of them, when, in fact, they lead nowhere. One's eye rests on the arches, failing to notice that the shadows they create conceal part of the boundary.

BRIDGES AND STEPS

A bridge over a natural stream or river, if you are lucky enough to have one, or spanning a pond, can make a strong centre to an outline design. One of the most effective I have seen is a wooden, Japanese hump-backed bridge in the

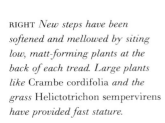

RIGHT *New steps have been softened and mellowed by siting low, matt-forming plants at the back of each tread. Large plants like* Crambe cordifolia *and the grass* Helictotrichon sempervirens *have provided fast stature.*

natural gifts should be treasured and incorporated into the overall design! In most cases, however, natural landscape features have to be contrived. Rock gardens are typical examples, and, for the keen plantsman, are essential.

▶ **Build a rock garden to create a natural landscape within an informal setting. Using stone and perhaps gravel you can construct one in a short time and plant it up instantly, choosing from a wide variety of readily available rock plants. You can add more interesting species later as the garden matures, if you like.**

▶ **Take advantage of something as simple as an old tree stump. Instead of uprooting what you might at first consider to be an eyesore, use it as the basis of a little wild garden. Plant it up with a collection of small species to flower at its feet and let ivy or honeysuckle scramble over the top. It will soon become a central feature of considerable interest and scope.**

▶ **Large *objets trouvés*, in the form of ancient, gnarled wood or pieces of water-sculpted stone make amusing features. To acquire these, though, you need a watchful eye, a capacious vehicle and a satisfactory explanation if you are caught 'lifting' from someone else's wild spot!**

LEFT *Made from disused telegraph poles, steps leading into a woodland garden emphasize a change in level. Because wood is often slippery when wet, the steps have been covered with chicken wire to give them grip.*

middle of an English garden in Wiltshire.

Steps, too, can make strong central features. A slope, a drop or indeed any difference in levels is a valuable asset in garden design, subdividing the area and thus increasing the interest quotient. A stairway through a gap in a wall draws attention to itself and, if it has to be there, is better made grandiose than understated!

▶ **Steps set into a change of level are all the better for a mantle of living plants on either side. If there is no room for them to be planted in the ground, set pots or containers on the steps or at their sides.**

NATURAL FEATURES

In the wild or informal garden, outline features might be natural, or can, at least, be made to look natural. Some gardens are blessed with outcrops of rock or interesting contours; such

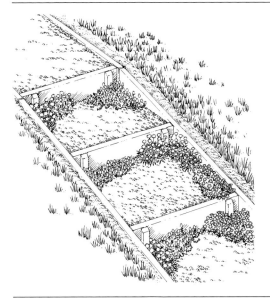

Steps can be built into sloping ground quickly and easily by cutting out a level area for each step and placing upright retaining boards fixed behind pegs and filling the cavities with gravel. The sides, too, need to be lined with board shaped to the slope. Take care, in grass, to recess the boards so that the top edges do not foul the mower.

RIGHT *A sculpture has rescued a dark grotto by focussing attention on it. Grottoes were loved by 19th-century gardeners, but to work in a modern setting, in a new garden, they need to be very thickly planted. Here, the luxuriant planting of different types of fern has taken advantage of the damp conditions.*

OPPOSITE *An amusing salute to the Roman style consists of a marble head on a plinth framed with a circular growth of golden hop. In winter, when the foliage will have died down, the statue will continue to be a focal point.*

SCULPTURE

Outline objects do not necessarily have to be large or impressive. Small or movable features can make useful, instant contributions. Numbers and arrangements are a matter of personal taste, of course, but it is usually better to place one or two with care than to scatter many about with gay abandon. Other traditional hardware such as obelisks or balustrades can be put to good use, as can modern sculpture.

▶ **Bring your garden to life, even before the plants have begun to mature, by carefully siting statues or sculpture.**

▶ Something as simple as a bird-feeding table, if well constructed, can make a worthwhile focal point. The design of an entire garden could radiate from a centrally placed dovecote, handsomely built either of painted timber or in stone and equipped with a thatched or slate roof.

▶ While your specimen trees are in their infancy, draw the eyeline in a different direction. Site pieces of sculpture or other *objets d'art* so that they make dominant features, taking the eye away from less well-developed areas. Parts of the garden viewed from the house, especially from rooms in frequent use, benefit from this.

TREES AND SHRUBS

ABOVE *Large trees and shrubs are easy to maintain in this established garden where interest has been heightened by growing oriental clematis over a gnarled tree.*

Helpful though man-made structures are, much of a garden's outline comes from living plants. Of these, trees and shrubs are the most permanent.

To say that trees are the slowest-growing of all plants is misleading. Just because a tree might take a century, or even more, to reach its ultimate height does not mean that it is slow, just big! But woody plants do vary enormously in the speed at which they grow and the slowest can frustrate your efforts to achieve early maturity. That does not mean that the fastest are necessarily the best to choose. Rapid shrubs can be coarse and leggy, or can look immature even though they get large quickly. These may be useful for a quick-growing shelter belt on the edge of the property. For the central part of the design, there is more to making the best selection than merely going for the fastest growers. We need artistic merit as well as speed.

Trees and shrubs come in a number of interesting shapes. Trees often have clear trunks, whereas shrubs have branches which go right to the ground. Conifers tend to be tapered from top to bottom. Deciduous trees often have spreading branches and rounded tops in maturity. There are wonderful exceptions whose limbs grow horizontally in tiers, like a wedding cake. Among garden trees, there are are also shapes known as columnar and fastigiate. Columnar trees develop into thick columns, usually tapering bluntly, rather than growing in a conical shape like a Christmas tree. Fastigiate varieties are decidedly tall and very thin. Such shapes are precious in the short-cut garden because the trees bring height quickly without taking up much space.

It is easy, in theory, to take a selection of the different plant shapes and arrange them into pleasing combinations. But in real life it is more difficult because the plants are living, growing, and therefore changing. What you are arranging is a set of potential shapes rather than a set of static objects, so you need to bear in mind what they will be like in a few years' time.

Although initial planting will be dense, it is important not to lose sight of the garden's ultimate outline. This means predicting how the garden is likely to look in five years' time. The specimen trees, the key shrubs and those special 'character' plants need to be carefully sited so that they fulfil their function as effectively in the mature garden as in the first few seasons. Then, when the time comes to do away with the short-term or interim plants, be ruthless and thin the planting severely until you are left with nothing but the long-term composition.

▶ The most attractive plantings are those with sculpted outlines where the eye is drawn towards the centre and upwards towards a high point. Making the tallest – or potentially tallest – trees the core point, around which all the other plants are assembled seems to make sense.

▶ It is also desirable to create interesting combinations of shapes with tall, thin plants placed so that lower ones nearby accentuate the contrast between their statures.

▶ Improve amorphous shrubbery or a collection of trees by planting something with striking characteristics so that it can stand out from among the general herbage. This is where the tree with tiered branches can be so useful.

Trees grow at their own pace and will not be hurried – but waiting is not on the short-cut gardener's menu!

▶ Resist the temptation to plant large, heavy standards or semi-mature trees. This is expensive, especially when the trees are so large they need handling with lifting equipment, and calls for diligent aftercare – including bracing and copious amounts of water for at least two seasons.

▶ Plant smaller, younger saplings – light standards and whips. Although these may

LEFT *For quick winter colour, Cornus alba, which comes in a variety of shades including red, black and yellow-green, forms a dense thicket of twigs within a couple of seasons, In the foreground, the variety is 'Flaviramea' and behind, the scarlet branches of 'Westonbirt' are just visible. To obtain twigs like these, the shrubs need to be cut back to the ground every year.*

Trees and shrubs can be grouped according to their typical shapes. Selections from each group can be made to work together to create a pleasing contour when planning any garden.
1   Fastigiate
2   Tiered
3   Conifer
4   Columnar
5   Typical deciduous
6   Shrub

look little more than twigs when they go into the ground, they will grow at an impressive rate, and will respond positively to feeding and cosseting

▶ If you are really impatient, you could place one or two extra-large trees in key positions, as anchor points, and flesh in the remainder of the planting with younger material which will take a season or two – or more – to develop.

SPEEDY LUXURIANCE

Things happen far more quickly with shrubs than with trees. A great many of them achieve at least a degree of maturity within a single season. Even the slow ones look attractive as soon as they have recovered from transplanting and begun to grow.

SPECIMEN TREES
Site these at key points

BUSHY SHRUBS
Fill out the profile

CHARACTER PLANTS
For shape and interest

WINTER COLOUR
Include evergreens of various shades

SHRUB ROSES
Best for speed with elegance

ABOVE *Built around a young tree, a simple pergola props up the branches forming a living parasol to shade the circular cast iron seat beneath.*

▶ Shrub roses are the best choice for combining speed with elegance. These are not the modern hybrid tea and cluster-flowered (floribunda) kinds, although they have their place too, but the bigger, more vigorous shrubby species and varieties. The one feature they almost all have in common is the ability to flower profusely on young wood which has bolted up to full height with staggering rapidity.

▶ The older varieties tend to come in soft pinks and wine reds, many having exquisite fragrance, and none of them requiring the rigmarole of pruning and spraying associated with modern breeds.

▶ Some shrub roses sport dazzling displays of autumn hips as well as summer blossom, others bloom continuously, or at the very least sporadically, throughout summer and every one of them has attractive foliage.

▶ The most rampageous shrub roses include such species as the red, single-flowered *Rosa moyesii* whose scarlet hips are flask-shaped; *R.* 'Highdownensis' which is similar but with pink blooms; *R. glauca* (syn. *R. rubrifolia*) and the sweet-briars, which have fragrant foliage. There are some glorious hybrid musk roses, which grow to generous proportions with

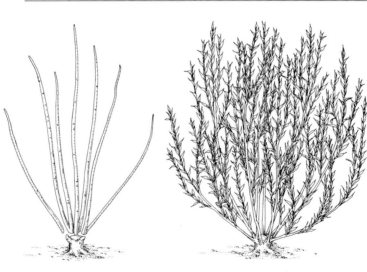

Many shrubs benefit from being cut right back to the ground once a year to within a bud or two of the old stump. The shrub will then grow vigorously, throwing up a mass of wands to make a large, rounded shape. Shrubs that respond particularly well to this brutal treatment are willow, *Prunus triloba*, *P. tenella*, all hazels, *Cotinus coggygria*, *Lonicera fragrantissima*, *Hydrangea paniculata*, *Physocarpus opulifolius*, forsythia (cut after flowering). You can cut most hardy shrubs back in autumn, but leave tender plants until spring.

surprising speed, and 'dual purpose' varieties, such as 'Maigold' and 'Scarlet Fire', which can grow freestanding into big, sprawling bushes or can be trained to a more sedate pattern on a wall. (The best and most useful short-cut roses are described on pages 122 and 127.)

▶ Fill your garden quickly by planting speedy shrubs, such as buddleias, some of which will grow more than 2.6m/8ft in a single season, *Lavatera thuringiaca* and *L. olbia* 'Rosea', which need a sunny position but flourish in drought. For spring and winter colour, *Kerria japonica* produces deep green canes spangled with small gold flowers.

▶ You can use willows to develop character speedily. The smaller species bring early maturity to a garden setting and can be made to look surprisingly elegant. Catkins, in a comprehensive range of subtle colours and textures from silvery satin to jet black, appear on young specimens and are in season in late winter and early spring, when they make particularly good companions for flowering bulbs planted beneath them.

Once you have installed a strong hard core of rapid developers, even the most short-term garden will look all the better for the addition of some architectural shrubs. Evergreens, which can give much to the body of the planting even while they are quite small, are particularly useful, and they sustain interest through the winter.

▶ For low, sculptural, evergreen shapes hebes, sarcococcas and daphnes are hard to beat. They seldom grow very large, but have mature shapes, often forming neat, rounded bushes.

▶ For bulk and sustained interest during winter, include some larger growing evergreens, such as hollies or laurels, in your planting plan.

No matter how careful you have been, within a year of two of planting, your shrubs are almost certain to look overcrowded. Indeed, as one of the secrets of a short-cut garden is dense

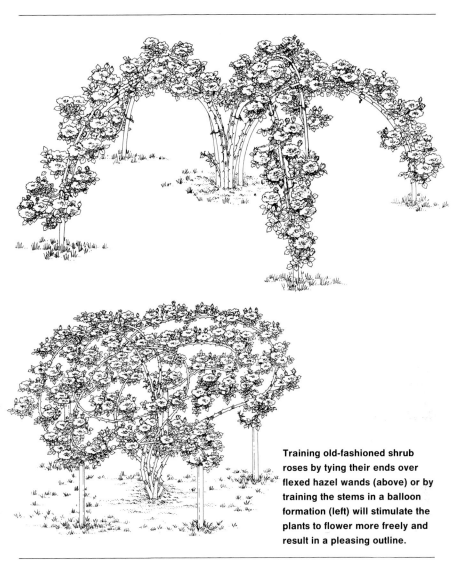

Training old-fashioned shrub roses by tying their ends over flexed hazel wands (above) or by training the stems in a balloon formation (left) will stimulate the plants to flower more freely and result in a pleasing outline.

planting in its early stages, thinning becomes a necessity, and will be the true test of your forward planning. If you got it right, the longer term shrubs should have become more dominant and be correctly spaced to fulfil their allotted role in the permanent outline. Thinning out the shrubs planted for the short term will be no more difficult than hardening your heart and being ruthless, even though you may have grown fond of them!

If you did not get your planning quite right, do not be dismayed. Shrubs do not object to being transplanted, particularly if you handle them carefully and provided you look to your aftercare. You may want to make adjustments for several seasons – most eminent gardeners do – and this is perfectly acceptable practice. Far better to play 'musical plants' than to be dissatisfied with the way your outline is arranged.

POTS AND CONTAINERS

Ivies or other evergreen creepers can be grown up a wire frame. Although they will closely resemble topiary they will reach their desired shapes in a third the time.

ABOVE *A group of containers planted with a mauve theme merge with the background to bring colour to a dark terrace.*

Containers are the short-cut gardener's boon. With arrangements of containers from large tubs bearing single trees, to troughs full of shrubs, to smaller pots and boxes crammed with herbaceous plants, you can transform a bare stretch of concrete paving into as floriferous and mature-looking a garden as one on a plot of the most perfect soil. Because they are instant, they can be enjoyed in the early days of a new garden while you wait for the rest of the plants to develop. But even in a garden that is well on its way to becoming established, containers are indispensable for use as focal points, to create height and as interesting decorative pieces in themselves.

▶ In a conventional garden, especially a new one or one newly renovated, you can install the first signs of maturity with a collection of containers.

▶ Soften the harshness of a new terrace or patio instantly by placing groups of generously planted pots or troughs on it or by it.

▶ Ring the changes as often as you like within any season with containers. This way you can bring in new pots as soon as an original planting has peaked, thus keeping up a constant sense of fullness and maturity.

Pots and containers can also be used in the same way as sculpture or other man-made objects except that they are more interesting because the plants they contain transform them into dynamic ornaments which change in character and appearance through the seasons.

▶ Provide positive focal points in a newly planted bed or border, which is almost always gappy at first, with some well-positioned urns or pots. These may be planted up, or left empty, as you wish.

▶ Use containers en masse, lined up and uniformly planted to make formal groups, either as boundary markers or to create special vistas.

ABOVE *Massed containers in an assortment of decorative stands have converted a covered patio area into a colourful garden.*

RIGHT *Assemblages of pots make quick features. A red theme here has been made up with the dahlia 'Bishop of Llandaff', assorted pelargoniums and the chocolate-scented* Cosmos atrosanguineus.

EARLY MATURITY
Install planted containers

SOFTEN HARSHNESS
Dress up terraces and patios

FOCAL POINTS
Fill in unsightly gaps

RING THE CHANGES
Keep up appearances

6

SHORT
CUTS TO
LAYOUT
DESIGN

As far as design is concerned, careful planning of the
three dimensional structure – the outline – is only one
short-cut route to the perfect garden. Layout is equally
important. Indeed, close attention to garden surfaces –
such items as pathways, terraces, paving and so on –
will reward you with quicker and more tangible
results than almost any other design aspect. Once you
have established your layout, the garden becomes
coherent. Then all that is left to be done is the
planting of the vegetation.

   This chapter discusses essential layout
considerations as well as many different kinds of
surface materials, including grass, that can be
employed.

A pattern of beds and pathways
has done much to establish the
character of a traditionally
designed kitchen garden. Layout is
the first consideration when
creating a new garden.

LAYOUT CONSIDERATIONS

ROOMY BORDERS
Encourage optimum speed and growth

RAISED BEDS
Increase design and planting possibilities

PLANT UP PATHS
Create a natural feel

ABOVE *Plants used as sculpture punctuate a paved courtyard at carefully measured intervals to create a formal design with a rigid structure.*

OPPOSITE TOP *Timber decking is a useful device for varying garden levels and surfaces. Once installed, it can be furnished with containers for an instant effect.*

OPPOSITE BOTTOM *A shaded spot for table and seats and intermittent areas of planting have been incorporated into this design which makes good use of old flagstones.*

In a small, private garden, you would be amazed at what a transformation can be effected by ensuring that the layout – borders, edges, lawns, pathways – has a definable structure.

A defined, measured layout looks permanent and gives the impression of being more established than a formless mass. Thus, a brand new garden begins to look established as soon as its layout has been set up. Even a task as simple as laying turf transforms a loose planting into a structured garden. Visit any big flower show and look at the exhibition gardens. Those that win the gold medals look as though they have been there for decades when, in fact, the finishing touches were probably being added with feverish haste just an hour or so before the public were allowed in!

What is the secret of those canny showmen? The answer is dense planting and 'finish'. At

Britain's Chelsea Flower Show, for example, the turf in the show gardens is rolled level, mown even, so that it has those soft stripes and looks no different from the 400-year old lawns of the Cambridge colleges!

In any layout there are certain features which, besides being good for the general design, contribute to a sense of maturity, either by speeding up plants or by creating an old-looking surface. Sometimes, in an established garden which needs renovating, there are several useful existing features such as walls, trees, paths or hedges that can be retained. These should be carefully evaluated since any or all of them could contribute much to the old feel of a newly overhauled garden (see pages 42–43), even if this means altering your layout and design to accommodate them. Often, they can be improved or their impact strengthened

For guidance, each garden element is given a short-cut rating to demonstrate just how effective it is likely to be. The rating is necessarily generalized because what works well as a short-cut strategy in one garden may not produce such good results in another.

★★★ Extra quick. Looks finished and mature within a single growing season or even sooner

★★ Quick. Bears some results in the first season and has reached a degree of maturity by the second

★ Moderately fast. Looks good in its second or third season

by simple adjustment to the layout that surrounds them. Pathways leading to trees which have been singled out as main features, close-mown rides through rough grass, or new borders set to flank existing hedges are all good examples.

Differences in level or other natural divisions within the garden all help to foster maturity, but it is the layout approaching these that will enhance the feeling more effectively. It is as important to accentuate positive features as it is to disguise or, at least, to dilute the effect of any negative aspects. Thus, eyesores such as manhole covers or the compost heap will need siting so that screens or disguising plants fit in with the rest of the layout.

Gardens change, of course, and it is unlikely that the initial layout is the one you will stick with for the rest of time. Having a fluid

ABOVE *A series of raised beds contained behind wooden boards gives quickly recognizable shape to a garden and evokes the ancient monastic style of physic garden where the planking was made of elm which is slow to rot.*

RIGHT *A thick carpet of pine needles, studded with planted islands, makes an atmospheric contribution to a Japanese-style garden. The oriental theme is reinforced by the graceful bamboo perimeter planting.*

approach enables you to maximize your potential for speedy maturity. Borders, for example, may well change in shape and size, as well as in content, during your garden's transformation from embryonic to established.

▶ Make sure that any new borders have dimensions, including soil depth, that are generous enough to ensure fast growth. To grow at optimum speed, plants need plenty of room, particularly for their roots. Small beds dry out more quickly than borders with generous proportions and are more difficult to enrich with compost or manure.

▶ Raised beds and borders increase interest and add that desirable ingredient, height. Even before planting, a system of raised beds exhibits a solid structure which helps to bind the design together. They can be quite charming and, in formal designs, they heighten the sense of geometry but allow plants to spill over their edges, softening rather than spoiling the line.

▶ Building up the levels of raised beds can be quite hard work, especially if they are more than 30cm/1ft high, but once made they will only require an annual top up of nourishing material – probably compost. You may have to import considerable quantities of topsoil at first, unless you draw from reserves in your own garden, perhaps creating a change in levels elsewhere.

▶ Raised beds provide a useful solution to the problems associated with water logging or infertility and are therefore ideal for areas where soil is poor and stony, or where drainage is inadequate.

▶ Raised beds enable you to widen your range of plants. If your soil is naturally chalky or alkaline, and you want to be able to enjoy camellias, azaleas or rhododendrons – none of which tolerates lime – raised beds filled with neutral or acid soil are the answer. But, in this case, you must prevent the soil in the raised bed from mixing with surrounding soil – a layer of thick plastic, laid on the surface before

building the raised bed will do this, but make sure the bed itself is free draining.

▶ By creating a pattern of raised plots and retaining the soil with timber planking, you could mimic the style of a mediaeval physic garden.

▶ If your pathways are wide enough, allow plants to spill over onto them, even to seed into them, to create a natural feel as well as to hasten that sought after, mature look. Encourage plant associations in borders to achieve a natural drift effect. There is no better way of fostering the illusion that the plants have spread themselves and that gives the impression of considerable age. Take care, though, not to overdo things – an undisciplined mass of plants can look unsightly.

ABOVE *As well as adding instant height and giving borders a sharply defined edge, raised beds ensure quick results by providing opportunities for the addition of extra soil.*

HARD SURFACES

HARMONIZE MATERIALS
Match new surfaces with existing
structures

SECOND-HAND GOODS
Build in maturity

SOFTEN NEW SURFACES
Plant up raw edges; encourage
mosses

PAVING PLANTS
Allow for planting holes when
laying surfaces

STEPPING STONES
Set concrete discs in gravel or
lawn

Surfaces are important because they influence
the texture, or feel, of a garden. Much can be
done with them to enhance the illusion of age
and maturity, but the wrong choice or style can
work the other way, resulting in a raw or
unfinished effect.

Those surfaces that enhance maturity are
usually old or old-looking. Anything that looks
too new – raw concrete, new paving slabs and
even clean-cut natural stone – should be
avoided if possible. If modern materials have to
be used, select those that are in sympathy with
their surroundings. Even crude concrete can be
made to look pleasant if it has taken on a colour
which blends with the building materials used
elsewhere in the garden.

Typical hard materials might include, in
decreasing order of 'matureness', old stonework,
old brick, new stonework, specially made
paving materials and ordinary concrete.

Old stonework ★★

Look for softer, old or weathered stonework, preferably covered with moss or lichens.

▶ **Flagstones with blurred edges and weathered and mellowed surfaces make a brand new yard or terrace look positively ancient in a few hours. Durability varies, of course, and prices, usually high, seem to relate to availability, rather than quality. Since almost all old material is preferable to new, however, take what you can get — well-worn stones which are hollowed and thin can often be reversed, laying the worn side down, in a bed of cement.**

Old brick ★★

Bricks make fine paving, being relatively easy to lay and having a soft effect. Aim to avoid fussiness and, if you are doing your own laying, stick to patterns which you know you can manage. Old bricks are often porous and, if perished, may have a limited life, particularly where they are likely to soak up moisture and then freeze and thaw, so pay attention to soundness when buying and laying them. To extend their life, they can be laid on a dry bed of hardcore or rubble, topped with a weak cement mix.

New stonework ★

New natural stone can look very classy right from the start and, if your pocket will run to it, runs a close second in choice to old natural stone. It is often less durable, however, and certainly takes its time to mellow. But in the long, term — when your garden ceases to be short cut and goes 'permanent' — you will be glad you laid natural stone and so, probably, will your successors!

ABOVE *Perennial plants — lavender, sea campions and pansies — flop over a loose arrangement of old flagstones softening the hard edges.*

OPPOSITE TOP *Old stone slabs, interplanted with grass, radiate from a huge, colourfully glazed vase, to make an eyecatching focal point.*

OPPOSITE BOTTOM *The green, giant leaves of a gunnera growing in a container dominate an arrangement of cobbles filling a tiny back yard. The riotous growth being encouraged around the boundaries has helped to soften the rather harsh effect of the new paving.*

OPPOSITE *Ranks of containers bring life and colour to a pathway of grey concrete slabs and soften the harsh edges.*

New brick ★

New bricks, manufactured especially for paving, are available in an ever-growing range of shapes and colours. Engineering bricks are much harder and more durable.

Concrete ★★

Concrete paving slabs are a mixed blessing and price does not necessarily relate to desirability. The cheapest, plain concrete slabs can often work as well as fancy, coloured or textured ones. Many that have been made to look old and weathered do not. Investigate as many of your suppliers as you can to see what is on offer. The better quality textured concrete products have natural stone, usually ground, on their surfaces and can look very convincing, especially when they have been down for a season or two. You can do a great deal to soften and mellow concrete, not just by treating it to encourage the spread of mosses and lichens but also by judicious planting.

▶ Encourage algae and, later, mosses to grow on new surfaces by treating them with dilute mixes of plant food. This works especially well in a damp climate. However, it is important to remember safety

You can make your own disc-shaped pavers quite easily. For a mould, cut – or ask a friendly mechanic to cut – an old 200l/40gall drum into 5cm/2in hoops. Cut through these once to make open, rather than closed, rings and tie them in the closed position with string. Set them out on pieces of rough board and fill them with concrete. Remove the pavers from the mould 48 hours after the concrete has set.

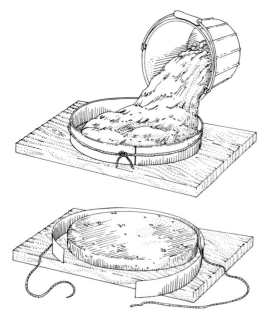

and probably better to keep surfaces that are destined to become thoroughfares as clean and as dry as possible

▶ However you plan your hard surfaces, do remember, when laying slabs, to leave gaps for planting or to make the gaps between slabs just wide enough to accommodate paving plants.

HOME-MADE PAVING

With sand, gravel, cement and makeshift moulds, you can craft paving slabs to whatever size you want for a fraction of the cost of manufactured ones. You also have far more choice of dimension and style, too. Large slabs may need reinforcing with welded mesh – easy to buy but you will need an angle grinder or a strong hacksaw to cut it – or with any old pieces of metal you might happen to have lying about.

▶ Break up gravel areas or lawns with pathways made of stepping stones, made quickly and cheaply *in situ*. Construct wooden moulds, place a little hardcore in the bottom, then pour cement over the top and texture the surface. In a lawn, set the tops of the stepping stones just below the level of the grass to avoid damaging the mower. The crunch of blade on concrete is a horribly expensive noise!

▶ Texture the surface of concrete as soon as you have poured it by incorporating grit or gravel onto it, then brush off the surplus once it has hardened. Setting cobble stones or old bricks into the concrete can have a softening effect and will help to foster the feeling of age, but your greatest ally in maturing cheap paving surfaces will always be time and the weather.

▶ To create an effect of natural, laid paving stone using concrete, set small strips of wood in a crossing pattern after pouring it. Remove these when it has almost set and brush the surface vigorously with a stiff bristle or wire brush to give a roughened surface with deep indentations which resemble flagstone paving, complete with gaps which you can fill later with compost and plant up with paving plants.

SOFT SURFACES

INSTANT SURFACE
Immediate results with gravel

VERSATILE GRAVEL
Choose colour and size to suit
your design

GREEN LAWN
Quick and inexpensive

ROUGH GRASS
Low maintenance and wildlife
friendly

ABOVE *Large-grade gravel has
been used as a quick, inexpensive
and effective surface. Concrete
slats have been added to turn the
gravel and planting into a feature.*

LEFT *A garden surface has been
made more interesting by laying
several different sizes of gravel
interspersed with large boulders
and brick dividers. The arid effect
is enhanced by semi-desert plants
such as agaves and echeverias.*

OPPOSITE *A gravel pathway
meandering through an informal
planting enables people to wander
among the plants. Gravel is in
perfect sympathy with the natural
theme here.*

GRAVEL ★★★

In a very small garden, or on a small section of a larger one, gravel is very useful as a soft surface. It is cheap, plants love growing in it, its maintenance is easy and it looks attractive. Perfect as a material for pathways, you can spread gravel further afield to incorporate planted areas.

Gravel is available in dozens of different textures, colours and sizes from sharp, milled grit to rounded river gravel. Choose the material which most closely matches your surroundings. In limestone areas, for instance, limestone chips are more likely to blend in than, say, granite pebbles.

▶ Gravel is quick and, provided you have a strong back, easy to install. You need a layer at least 5cm/2in thick, which you may have to top up from time to time, particularly if the soil beneath is soft, causing the gravel to become mixed up with it. Its one serious drawback is that it is difficult and expensive to remove should you change your mind about it.

▶ Use gravel to create instant pathways or car parking areas.

▶ Lay it as a substitute for a lawn; this is especially useful in a tiny garden, or a small area of a larger one.

▶ Use contrasting coloured gravels to create interesting design effects.

▶ You can use gravel as an attractive mulch for flower borders, where it will help to retain valuable moisture.

▶ Gravel is useful for a rock garden where it can be laid to form a natural-looking scree.

▶ Plant up a wide gravel pathway to look as if plants in the border have spilled naturally into it. Bulbs, even quite large ones like tulips or narcissus, can be planted in drifts across the line of the border into the gravel pathway. This device softens hard lines, thus adding to the illusion of age. Alternatively, plant the path with its own special plants.

MOWN GRASS ★★

Besides borders, pathways and paving, most gardens have a significant area laid down to a soft surface, usually lawn. In the short-cut garden, a lawn is a quick and relatively inexpensive way to acquire maturity, so it is worth sparing a moment or two to see how lawns, or rather 'grass', can be put to work.

Fashions are changing. The concept of a weedless, uniform grass sward is, nowadays, seen by fewer people as the perfect lawn. The concept of regular and copious dosing with weedkiller and mineral fertilizer is no longer universally acceptable, and to the organic gardener it is anathema. In the light of our more ecologically minded age, we must re-define the subject. A perfect lawn, for today, is one which stays green and healthy throughout the year so that it can support wear and tear from feet, footballs, spilled martinis and dropped barbecue fuel, but which looks good enough to enhance the remainder of the garden.

Weeds, or rather wild flowers, on our modern-day perfect lawn are to be tolerated – encouraged even – and the number of different grass species which make up the body of the turf are far more varied than before. But weeds, if they threaten the health and spread of the grass, reducing the lawn's hard-wearing qualities, do need controlling, as do coarse grasses which ruin a fine lawn's texture.

The extent to which you tolerate lawn weeds will depend on the formality of your garden and on your preferences. My own grass is studded with any number of small, rosette-forming plants such as daisies, self heal and plantains, but I must confess I do still apply weedkiller about every fourth year to prevent the more invasive weeds such as yarrow (*Achillea mille-folium*) from destroying the grass.

Small lawns or areas of grass can be trouble-some to look after and may contribute less to your garden than an alternative surface such as gravel or paving.

ROUGH GRASS ★★

If you have the room, and if you are interested in creating a haven for wildlife, an area of rough grass, far from spoiling a garden, can be an interesting feature. It could be the ideal soft surface for a wild garden, a small, waste corner

which does not fit in with the rest of your design, or even a little orchard. With or without naturalized flowers, a rough grass area attracts butterflies and wild birds, and looks natural and long-established very quickly.

▶ You can contrive a flower meadow, which in nature might take hundreds of years to evolve, within a couple of seasons. Wild species are widely available both as seed and as plants and, once established, will be self-perpetuating. How rich in numbers of species your flower meadow will be, depends on soil type and natural local flora as much as on the plants you introduce. Poor soil tends to perform better than rich and the golden rule is never to feed wild flowers.

Close-mown pathways allow access into rough grass areas without invading the wildlife territory. The smallest flowers, which would go unnoticed in a real meadow, stand out along the edges of the close-mown areas. Close mowing round groups of shrubs in otherwise long

meadow grass also aids maintenance by improving accessibility and preventing the long grass from growing up into the shrubs and spoiling their appearance.

Close-mown strands running through otherwise rough pasture may be a fine short-cut technique and is so undemanding on maintenance as to be the lazy gardener's dream, but even long grass needs at least one annual cut. Failure to do that would result in a gradual takeover by wild shrubs and trees. Furthermore, the grasses themselves would become tussocky and coarse.

▶ Where there is space, the technique of having close-mown 'rides' or pathways through rough grass produces some exciting results. Using the paths to mark boundaries for the wilderness gives even the most unkempt of gardens a groomed appearance. With clever siting, the close-mown paths can lead the eye to distant prospects – a shapely clump of trees, perhaps, a group of brightly flowering shrubs or, in a seriously grand garden, a gazebo or even a folly!

ABOVE *A close-mown pathway leads through a flower meadow to a boundary gate. Grass paths are easy on the eye and surprisingly hard wearing, except where there is constant trampling.*

OPPOSITE TOP *In wildlife-friendly gardens lawn and flowerbeds can merge, allowing meadow flowers like daisies and buttercups to thrive in the grass. Meadows take more managing than close-mown lawns and the kinds of flower that will thrive in them depends on the length of time between cuts.*

OPPOSITE BOTTOM *The lawn, which makes a central feature, brings together the luxuriant planting schemes in the borders. In a new site, laying a turf lawn has the immediate effect of turning a half-developed plot into an identifiable garden.*

7

SHORT CUTS WITH POOLS AND PONDS

Water is the stuff of life. From the biological point of view, every living being needs it to survive. From the artistic point of view, water adds a special extra ingredient that can be the making of a garden. A great many designers refuse to contemplate a garden plan without water and frequently it plays a central role in their landscapes. But, like all hard landscape features, water can be overdone and an insensitive or self-indulgent designer may ruin a good thing by having too many water courses, fountains and pools.

Yet, a garden with water is almost always more interesting than one without. Water features provide another key to an established feel. Although sometimes costly, they are quick and easy to install, and can be designed to suit every imaginable style of garden from a natural wildlife pool to a Persian-style rill that might grace a harem.

Well stocked with aquatics and surrounded by handsome foliage plants, water makes an alluring feature. A pond has a beneficial effect on a garden's ecology.

WATER ATTRACTION

Perhaps because it is at the very core of our being, water has a fascination. Children are drawn to it like bees to nectar, loving to dabble their bare feet in its coolness or float sticks on its surface. Among adults, it provides therapy for the weary – there is a restful quality about staring into limpid depths – and a whole range of extra activities for the energetic gardener. As far as wildlife is concerned, bodies of water have their own special ecology. As well as the interesting plants and animals that live in or near ponds or streams, there are lots of dryland species which will be attracted into a garden just to make use of the water.

The enriching quality of a pond is best illustrated by the experience of a colleague. Having dug the hole the weekend before, he toiled all one Saturday, laying out the butyl liner, levelling the sides and then filling the new pond. Even before the pond had filled to the brim, a large dragonfly appeared from nowhere, hovered over the water for a minute or two and then began to dip its abdomen to the surface film to lay eggs. The wildlife colonization of this new habitat had thus begun within minutes of completing the project.

Apart from its interest for naturalists, a water feature provides a focal point with a change of mood. Waterfalls, streams and fountains make movement which sparkles in the sunshine; still waters change dimensions by reflecting trees and buildings in their surfaces. Water reflects the sky, too, changing the quality of light in the garden and therefore altering the appearance of neighbouring plants.

As for planting schemes, water presents a fascinating range of new opportunities. Water plants tend to grow large quickly, with big, exotic-looking foliage and conspicuous flowers. Within a season, the margin of a pond or stream can acquire an appearance of great age. The water ecology also develops quickly, as far as the plants are concerned, although it takes a few years to become fully developed. It is all a question of achieving the right balance so that growth of algae, which clouds water or turns it green, is suppressed. Ways in which this 'balance' can be achieved in the pond are covered on page 102.

SETTING UP A POND

In the short-cut garden, the pond is such an excellent means of providing interest quickly that not to install one would be casting off a valuable opportunity.

The hardest part is digging the hole. You may discover bedrock you did not know you had or encounter a stony subsoil which will be perilous for the liner unless you remove all sharp edges, including tree roots. To protect the pond liner it is worth going to the trouble of spreading a layer of damp sand onto the sides and bottom and laying an outer liner before installing the butyl. Check the whole site carefully for nobbles or bumps caused by missed pebbles or other hard objects – as these could puncture the skin – and make sure there are no wrinkles or kinks in the liner. It is also worth double checking your levels. Care must be taken to ensure that edges of the pond are dead level so that none of the liner shows and so that the water sits where you expect it to.

The length of a liner needs to be the overall length of the pond plus twice the maximum depth. Its width will be the pond's overall width plus twice the maximum depth.

▶ **A pond can be finished either by constructing paving around its edges or by burying the edges of the liner under turf. The soil from the hole can be used to create a surrounding landscape, perhaps for an informal setting, or used elsewhere.**

▶ **Add a fountain, waterfall or stream to a pond to add interest and to keep the environment healthy by mixing oxygen into the water. Any fish and other life forms will benefit, as will green plants at night when they are not manufacturing their own oxygen – a good reason, in hot weather for having the fountain, stream or trickle running all night!**

ABOVE *A pond with a Japanese theme includes a devil-catching bridge, assorted round boulders and, in the background, a fountain for ablutions.*

LEFT *Surrounded by quick-growing greenery a small stone bowl makes a focal point. Water benefits even the most restricted of gardens.*

INFORMAL WATER FEATURES

ABOVE *A well-designed wildlife pond merges with the thick vegetation that surrounds it. Massed aquatic plants, in this case European natives, lend an air of authenticity and provide cover for wild creatures.*

OPPOSITE TOP *In a large natural pond, aquatics and marginal plants such as water lilies,* Iris laevigata, Euphorbia griffithii *and sedges can be allowed to form huge clumps.*

OPPOSITE BOTTOM *Gently sloping sides look natural and enable birds, insects and amphibians to go in and out of the water with ease. Where the pond is made from a butyl liner, rounded cobbles help to create the desired finish.*

Apart from the lucky few who enjoy natural water resources in their gardens, the majority of water features are entirely artificial. But the scope for a truly natural appearance is almost as wide as with natural water.

▶ Use a butyl liner to mimic nature at an affordable cost – you can make your butyl-lined pond as big as you like. Ponds specifically designed to encourage wild-life need at least one shallow, sloping side, preferably extended to a wet area. The liner, in this shallow zone, can be masked by arranging rounded cobbles or by placing soil or turf over it.

▶ Getting the depth right in relation to surface area is important to achieve an ecological balance in a natural pond as quickly as possible. Generally a surface area of 2.5-9.5sqm/25-100 sqft requires a maximum depth of 45cm/18in; 9.5-18.5sqm/100-200sqft requires 60cm/24in maximum depth; and anything over 20sqcm/200sqft needs 75cm/30in.

▶ Shape the hole so that there is a shelf all round the edges, roughly 22.5cm/9in below the surface of the water to take marginal plants. Plant up baskets with the marginal plants and stand them on the shelf.

The most desirable water feature is a truly natural watercourse. If your garden has a stream or a pond in it, rejoice at your good luck. If it has a soggy hollow, dig! You may discover a water feature you did not know you had!

With natural water, the task of the gardener is merely to get the most out of the resource by trying to enhance nature without spoiling it. Large rivers or streams usually make up their own minds about where they want to go and altering their course requires heavy engineering works. Tiny brooks or trickles are more malleable, however, and can be dammed, diverted, encouraged to meander, deepened, widened and so on. The most natural-looking water garden will probably consist of series of pools connected by trickles or streamlets.

▶ Provided it is bedded in an impervious clay soil or the ground dips below the natural water table you can influence the size and shape of a natural pond. Little bays and inlets provide special planting features; large shallow areas widen the scope for a wildlife-friendly wetland.

Natural-looking streams are less easy to contrive on a large scale, because, to give the appearance of flowing, the water needs to be pumped. But it is not difficult to make a little water movement go a long way. There are dozens of ways in which water can be used imaginatively, though. Think, for example, of a chain of little pools in varying sizes and shapes, all connected by streams or necks of still water to mimic a natural wetland scene. Bubbling springs, where water does little more than cascade up and over a group of large stones – a useful safety feature for a garden where very young children might be at risk – are easy to install and make a delightful focal point for an informal planting.

▶ Place rocks and pebbles to help conjure up the image of a babbling brook – use them to divert the flow of pumped water. Plant small shrubs to hang gracefully over

the stream and add creeping plants to clothe the 'banks' right down to the water's edge.

►Create a stream by pumping water uphill and allowing it to cascade down into a pond that is as large as you can afford (in terms of space as well as budget). Improve the stream with careful attention to the banks and sides – vary its width, make it meander a little and hold it up with rocks, little weirs or level changes which cause tiny rapids. That way, the running water takes on a high profile. The still, deep waters of the pool at the end provide contrast, with large marginal plants, fish and perhaps even statuary used to evoke an atmosphere of mystery.

►By adding a small waterfall at one end you can make even a simple pond, no more than 3m × 2m/9ft × 6ft, very natural look-ing. Fed by a tiny pump, even a small trickle is enough to enliven the scene and will also aerate the water.

ENHANCE A NATURAL FEATURE
Landscape a pond or stream

MIMIC NATURE
Create a natural-looking feature

CREATE A BROOK
Pump water

LIVEN UP A POOL
Add a waterfall

FORMAL WATER FEATURES

ABOVE *A formal pond in a garden has been planted with a white theme. With such a small volume of water, plant selection needs to be judicious and planting sparse, giving pride of place to the water itself.*

OPPOSITE *A little cascade provides a semi-shaded corner with movement and sound. Filling the basin with stones rather than a pool of water makes this cooling feature safe for young children.*

In the short-cut garden, formal water features are especially useful because they work well with very sparse planting – and are therefore effective quickly. A long, rectangular pond, for example, might need nothing more than a strategic clump of irises, for instance, and a dozen water lily leaves and flowers. Such planting would look good within a few months of being introduced, because much of the 'life' would be brought to the site by water which is instant, rather than by plant growth which takes longer.

▶ **Add grace and movement to a formal setting. Styles vary widely to suit all tastes: from a circular pond with fountains; to a half moon feature running up to a wall from which water flows; or a series of straight, narrow watercourses (rills) set in line with the architecture of a house or following the edge of a terrace; or, perhaps, nothing more than a square or rectangular pond as centre to a square or rectangular terrace or patio.**

▶ **If space is limited or you do not want to install a pond, you can still enjoy a water feature. Large stone jars or waterproof tubs make excellent vehicles for water gardens in miniature, many of which can even accommodate fish!**

▶ **On a slightly larger scale, rather than digging holes, ponds can be held in retaining walls, perhaps incorporated in a raised bed or simply as a raised tank. Care needs to be taken with design, otherwise it might look too much like a functional water cistern but, by furnishing the sides cunningly and with thoughtful siting, a raised pond can be surprisingly effective.**

In a formal garden, the pond is likely to be geometrically shaped, probably with straight or rounded margins and usually set into formal terraces or lawns. It is the line of the water feature that matters here, rather than a natural look or the planting.

Although no attempt is made to imitate natural streams or watercourses in formal water features, they can have plenty of grace and movement. These are achieved with fountains or other contrivances and by the choice of position for the water feature. Formal designs can instill feelings of tranquillity, usually because the water is still and the pools are positioned to reflect buildings and sky. Mountain streams would hardly fit in a formal arrangement but flowing stairs, narrow runnels of stonework, and large-volume, low-pressure fountains can all be used to bring the artificial landscape to life.

The most difficult water feature of all to harmonize in any garden setting is a swimming pool. The garish blue of some of the building or lining materials, the straight-sidedness, the outbuildings that always seem to have to go with them, even the stench of chlorine, make swimming pools a dubious asset for the serious gardener. They take a lot of looking after too, not to mention the spate of uninvited guests they elicit! But, if you have one, it has to be neutralized somehow by careful siting and by even more careful planting.

BRINGING WATER TO LIFE

OXYGENATE WATER
Keep water healthy

SHADE THE SURFACE
Broad-leaved plants

IMITATE WETLAND PLANTING
Grow lush-leaved plants on dry margins

USE ARTIFACTS
Create an established feel early on

ADD A FOUNTAIN
Keep water on the move

ABOVE *A raised pond provides an attractive alternative where excavation would be difficult. In so small a space, the plants must work hard to justify their placing.*

OPPOSITE *Long, thin water features like this rill, with formal planting alongside, increase the potential for interesting reflections.*

For water to work properly, not just as part of a well-designed garden, but as a haven for wildlife, and a favourable habitat for plants, it is necessary for it to be ecologically balanced. This is merely a matter of keeping the water, even if it does not flow or move, fresh and sweet. It is easy to know when your pond is not balanced — the water stinks! It may also be cloudy, or green with suspended algae, or stiffened and stringy with blanket weed. These, though unsightly, are less troublesome than stinking, stagnant water. The main causes of imbalance are a lack of dissolved oxygen, an excess of dissolved nitrogen salts and too much direct sunlight.

▶ Encourage plenty of oxygenating plants (water weed) to grow. Any of the common river weeds — *Elodea canadensis, Ceratophyllum demersum* or the white-flowering water crowfoot (*Ranunculus aquatilis*).

▶ Grow plants with good-looking, broad, floating leaves to provide shade on the water's surface. Water lily leaves are the most obvious choice, but there are others, equally delightful. The water hawthorn (*Aponogeton distachyos*), for example, has oval, floating foliage and curious creamy-white, fragrant flowers.

▶ Nitrogen is usually caused by the polluting effect of excreting fish or by nitrates already dissolved in added water. You can counter this by growing plenty of nitrogen-hungry green plants in the water. Oxygenating weeds themselves help enormously but plants like water hyacinth (*Eichornia crassipes*), which multiply at an amazing pace in summer, literally gobble up pollutants. Unfortunately, the water hyacinth is not hardy but it can be overwintered in an indoor aquarium. It has built-in flotation chambers and is fun to grow.

Most of a water feature's maturity comes from the plants themselves.

▶ Wetland species are naturally big and soft. Large, broad leaves on plants like *Rheum palmatum* or *Ligularia dentata* contribute a lot of vegetation early on.

►Irises are wonderful for lush growth, filling out with their sword-like foliage in rapid time and doubling up by reflecting themselves in the water.

►Other speedy plants include many of the grasses, sedges and their near relatives, the bamboos. These need careful placing, since the needle-sharp young shoots could pierce the butyl liner and cause a leak, but they look gorgeous arching over a pond. In the breeze, their movement is graceful and their outline dramatic but it is important to match size to site.

►You can create the illusion of a marshy, damp area around a man-made pond surprisingly quickly by planting up the dry margins with lush plants. The hosta is a great ally here, thriving in an ordinary border but looking as though it is revelling in marshy ground near a pond. *Iris pallida* 'Argentea Variegata' is also useful and has a similar appearance to the fine, silver-variegated form of *Iris laevigata*.

►Encourage trees to 'weep' over water-courses and trailing shrubs to tumble between rocks or down steep banks to further the illusion of wetland.

►In a small pool, plant aquatics in baskets and distribute these along the pond's shelf. Grown this way, they are easy to move about, to replant and to transfer between ponds. Use a specially prepared compost to hasten their growth.

►Plant water lilies in large tubs or special lily baskets and gently lower these to the bottom of the deepest part of the pond. You will need a helper for this task.

For more information on suitable plants to grow in and around ponds, refer to page 129.

►Until your pool matures, use artifacts — containers, weathered rocks, old garden furniture — to create an established look.

►Elegant fountains make up for a deficit of flora. Nowadays, aquatic specialists carry a bewildering range of statuary and fountainheads.

8

SHORT CUTS TO PLANTING SCHEMES

Up to this point, we have looked chiefly at how design and layout can be used to maximize the speed at which the garden can acquire a developed look. Now it is time to get down to some specific examples. This chapter looks at a selection of fairly typical garden sites and provides them with planting recipes for quick development.

The suggestions are by no means hard and fast but are offered as a stimulus for your own ideas rather than a planting blueprint. They show what can be done, rather than what should be done, and any variation on the theme which you think might be better for your own situation probably will be better, so give it a try!

A moist woodland floor planted
with a largely green theme,
restrained use of variegated foliage
and wild flower species sets a
tranquil mood.

OPPOSITE *Cranesbill,* Knautia macedonica *and betony, speedy perennials with lasting colour and great staying power, work together in a delightful pink planting. On the brick wall behind,* Clematis viticella *'Etoile Violette' will scramble to 2.6m/8ft or more in a single summer, even though it is cut to ground level every spring.*

Each planting scheme in this chapter is assessed for speed of development as well as the amount of time it will require for maintenance. In practice, growth rates vary according to your local conditions – climate, aspect, soil etc – but results will always be faster where optimum conditions are provided. Even the hastiest of gardens, therefore, will depend on good husbandry to perform well.

Although no two planting situations are exactly alike, there are some basic considerations that are common to them all. So when adapting any of the following recipes to suit your own garden arrangement, keep these in mind. The aim is to create a specific mood and to do this you will need several common themes.

Colour is important. In addition to the colours you plant, you will need to consider contrasts or colour harmonies. A yellow theme, for example, can use variegated or golden foliage as well as flowers.

Textures should contrast, too. And you must pay attention to heights and spreads so that the plants are assembled together comfortably.

But, since this is a short-cut garden, as well as all these aesthetic aspects, you will need to select for speed.

THINNING OUT A BORDER
Dense initial plantings will need adjusting within a couple of seasons. High speed shrubs such as tree mallow, flowering currant and buddleia (top) will need removing to make room for choicer plants that will by then have grown much larger and need to develop their shape without inhibition (bottom). Similar treatment is necessary for herbaceous plants, reducing rampant populations of red valerian, foxgloves and alchemilla, for instance, to allow more space for choice plants such as hostas and other more sedate plants.

The planting schemes have been devised for the most rapid development possible in the conditions, but in most cases, would be appropriate for the long term as well. Speed of development varies from site to site and so each example is given a star rating, intended as a very rough guide to how soon you can expect tangible results.

★★★ Extra quick.
Looks finished and mature within a single growing season

★★ Quick.
Bears some results in the first season and reaches a degree of maturity by the second

★ Moderately fast.
Looks good in its second or third season

Maintenance is also a major consideration here and so each of the schemes is graded according to the amount of weeding, feeding, propagating and so on you can expect to have to do to keep it looking good.

★★★ Minimal maintenance once established – an occasional run through to remove weeds

★★ Moderate maintenance required, plus some regular development work, such as hedge trimming, but nothing too arduous

★ Labour intensive. Benefits from minor attention every few days and major replanting at least once a season

A HOT SPOT GARDEN

SHORT CUT RATING ★★★

MAINTENANCE ★★★

ASPECT
Thin, very free-draining soil which
tends to dry out. Full sunshine

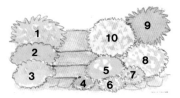

A semi-desert can be made to
bloom when Mediterranean and
other dryland species are
planted. Extra flowers can come
from spring, summer and autumn
bulbs.

1   Intermediate bearded iris
2   Nasturtium
3   *Genista hispanica*
4   *Helianthemum*
5   *Allium christophii*
6   *Convolvulus cneorum*
7   Verbena
8   *Cistus ladanifer*
9   *Yucca gloriosa*
10 *Cistus purpureus*

Outline plants in these conditions need little
attention once they have become established.
Slow-growing they may be but they still make
good short-cut plants because they look attractive from the moment they are planted. Small
conifers such as *Juniperus communis* or the little
dwarf pine *Pinus sylvestris* 'Watereri' make
useful architectural plants, as pretty in mid-
winter as at any other time of year. Summer
shrubs include the rockroses, especially evergreen *Cistus ladanifer* and *C. × corbariensis*.

Daisy bushes (olearia) are good value for dry
spots, not just for the avalanche of white
blossom in summer but also for their leathery,
evergreen leaves. These look well in the
company of silver foliage – a widespread and
attractive characteristic of sun-loving plants,
particularly Mediterranean natives. One of the
choicest is *Convolvulus cneorum* which gleams
with an almost metallic silver sheen and has
exquisite saucer flowers, white with a hint of
pink in the bud.

Planted among the silvers, arid-loving bulbs
will make a delightful display in their first
season and will multiply thereafter. Many of
the onion tribe (alliums) are especially good at
this, producing clusters of brightly coloured
flowers in early summer, often following them
with handsome seed heads. Quickest and easiest
of the big performers is *Allium christophii* (syn.
A. albopilosum).

For late winter and spring, massed plantings
of crocuses, especially the smaller species such

as the golden yellow *Crocus ancyrensis* and the
dozens of delightful forms of *C. chrysanthus*,
will give a heartwarming display and will also
multiply steadily.

In high summer, there are plenty of tender
species which can be popped into gaps to beef
up colour and bulk up on the living material.
Petunias are utterly commonplace but there is
nothing wrong with that! Verbenas love hot
spots, too, and come in many shades.

As well as tender varieties, a scattering of the
more drought-resistant hardy annuals will help
here, especially in the first season when the
more permanent plants are in their infancy.
Field poppies, though they become troublesome in fertile soil, are quite happy growing
in near-starving conditions. Other drought-
tolerant annuals include Californian poppies
(eschscholzia) and the rapid growing nasturtium *Tropaeolum majus*.

For extra hot, dry sectors where there is little
or no soil at all, there are still fine plants which
relish such conditions from the delicate-
flowered but tough-growing dwarf *Iris pumila*
to those extraordinarily resilient survivors the
stonecrops. *Sedum acre*, for example, makes a
little golden carpet of flowers in spring and
follows with mossy foliage but if you need
something larger, try one of the tougher yuccas.
Yucca filamentosa seems to be one of the most
drought resistant but *Y. gloriosa* is more
sensational with its huge spires of delightful
cream flowers.

A GARDEN IN DRY SHADE

SHORT CUT RATING ★★

MAINTENANCE ★★★

ASPECT

Typical town garden site, shaded by trees and tall buildings but on reasonable soil. Some parts gets direct sunshine for a small part of the day

Among shrubs, there are plenty of drab, boring evergreens that will thrive in dry shade but of course, we want more than that! Nevertheless, we will be depending on a hardcore of relatively unexciting evergreens to provide background and a winter outline.

The much maligned *Aucuba japonica* – scorned because it is so over planted in difficult, gloomy sites, has a great deal to contribute. In conjunction with other plants, it provides dependable greenery all year, and, if you select female clones, has bright red, long-lasting berries as well. Probably the most commonly grown variety is the stipple-leaved 'Crotonifolia', a non-fruiting male which makes a good companion to the female 'Salicifolia' which has sea-green stems and a heavy crop of berries.

For flowers in dry shade, the mahonias are worthwhile. *Mahonia japonica* is unsurpassable for its sweet scent and winter flowers, but the more tender species *M. lomariifolia* grows taller and has more erect flower stems. *Mahonia × media* is a popular hybrid of which the most widely grown is 'Charity' but the finest form of all is 'Lionel Fortescue'.

The viburnums are a useful group of speedy plants for dry shade. The evergreen *Viburnum tinus* flowers on very young plants and very prettily too, especially the pink-budded *V. tinus* 'Eve Price'. There is a cream, variegated form, slow-growing, but excellent in good soil. *Viburnum davidii* is lower growing and has nicely textured, deep green leaves, making a lovely foil for herbaceous plants or other low shrubs with contrasting leaves.

Pale colours show up best in the gloom so, when choosing summer shrubs for their flowers, go for white, pale pink, cream or pale yellow. Species of pieris, in acid soil, will tolerate moderate shade and have generous clusters of white or pink flowers which look like tiny Chinese lanterns. The young shoots of *Pieris* 'Forest Flame' are vermilion.

Among herbaceous plants, one of the finest for dry shade is lily of the valley (*Convallaria majalis*). As a weed-suppressing ground cover, it has no equal in dry shade and, as a cut flower, it is surely one of the prettiest and most sweetly scented. There are several forms. The North American woodland species *Smilacina racemosa* is an excellent plant for dryish shade, but will not tolerate extended drought. The feathery cream flowers are held at the ends of the arching stems. Similar in foliage, if not in flower, are the Solomon's seals. Together with lily of the valley, these plants will make an attractive, low-maintenance carpet. Pepper this with the purple-leaved *Viola labradorica purpurea* and the softly marbled foliage of *Tolmiea* 'Taff's Gold' and you have the makings of a fine, and quick-developing plant association.

Few summer bedding plants put up with these conditions but impatiens is the most shade-tolerant of all. In good soil or compost, this will flower in gloomy conditions and comes in most shades from deep red to white.

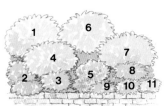

Dense foliage and pale flower colours help to alleviate the symptoms of dry shade. Evergreens, since so many of them grow naturally on dry woodland floors, are especially useful.

1 *Mahonia japonica*
2 *Tiarella cordifolia*
3 *Polygonatum multiflorum*
4 *Viburnum davidii*
5 *Pieris forestii*
6 *Aucuba japonica* 'Crotonifolia'
7 *Viburnum tinus*
8 *Smilacina racemosa* (False spikenard)
9 Lily of the valley
10 Impatiens
11 *Tolmiea menziesii*

A GARDEN OF ANNUALS

SHORT CUT RATING ★★★

MAINTENANCE ★★

ASPECT
A well lit, sheltered garden with reasonable – but not rich – soil in a climate which has prolonged frost periods in winter.

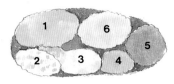

Tender perennials, often grown as annuals in cold climates, provide a colourful short-cut display. Pelargoniums, penstemons and the many different salvia species are all valuable plants and are easy to overwinter under glass as young rooted cuttings. They can grow from these to flowering size in less than a month and then bloom continuously until late autumn.

1. *Cosmos atrosanguineus*
2. Verbena hybrids
3. Penstemon
4. *Pelargonium crispum* 'Variegatum'
5. *Amaranthus*
6. *Salvia sclarea*

From the short cut point of view, an annual garden is speedy in its development and so can make a superb interim solution while other, more permanent projects are under way. Planning for a certain amount of succession will prevent an over-blown appearance in late summer. But annual gardens do tend to be seasonal and there will always be a drab period in winter.

The better the conditions, the better the display but even if the soil and lighting fall short of the ideal, it is not too difficult to come up with a planting recipe that will still work. To make the plants grow with vigour, the soil should be well worked and improved with compost and feed. Regular watering in dry conditions helps further.

Most hardy annuals can be sown directly into the ground in autumn or spring. Autumn-sown plants usually grow larger and flower for longer than spring-sown ones, but will be over sooner. A balance of spring and autumn sowing is therefore probably the safest bet.

Thinking in terms of colour schemes, one of the charms of so many annuals is their kaleidoscopic effect, so one can afford to be swashbuckling when it comes to dreaming up schemes. Certain combinations are especially breathtaking. The sharp orange of pot marigolds (calendulas) contrasts gloriously with the deep blue of larkspurs or cornflowers. Pink mallow looks heavenly grown behind a lavender hedge and harsh reds make a floral counterpoint for the rusty hues of autumn daisies such as rudbeckias. Mauve and cream go together happily, especially if there is silver foliage, so a group of *Collinsia grandiflora* might be just the plants to associate with feverfew, *Chrysanthemum coronarium* 'Primrose Gem' or perhaps creamy white candytuft – especially the pretty species *Iberis amara*. Finally, for a touch of the mysterious, try black flowers! The little viola 'Bowles Black' is the colour of boot polish and makes a fascinating contrast with deep red or with green flowers such as *Moluccella laevis*.

With all these flowers, interesting foliage is an essential ingredient, not only smoothing down any harshness caused by massing of colours but also tying the planting together. Annuals which have pretty foliage are fairly few and far between but in certain species, the flower/leaf combination works really well. The broad furry foliage of *Salvia argentea* is ideal for sunny sites and, although its flower spikes are unimpressive, it should be allowed to seed as it will self-sow in the right conditions. Nigella is as worthwhile for its lacy foliage and strange seed heads as for its pretty blue flowers, and has a wonderfully cooling effect.

The success of an annuals garden really depends on thoughtful planning. Some have a long flowering season, others provide shorter bursts of brilliant colour. Some are best in late spring, others sport conspicuous seed capsules in autumn. A combination of as many different

characteristics as possible helps to lengthen the season and add interest but there is always the danger, if your selection is too catholic, of ending up with a formless mess! If you can visualize the result of your seed sowing, you are half way to good planning but if not, pay close attention to the habits, ultimate heights and compatibility of the plants you have chosen so that you are able to put them together for the most effective results.

To save on time and trouble, keep to a minimum the number of varieties that will need staking or supporting. An effective way of planning with annuals is to divide the border, or borders, up into blocks or divisions and then to note down, not necessarily specific plants for these but rather, the characteristics you would like to see. Thus, you might want a blue and pink theme in one area, with silver foliage in between the colours. In another part, you may want more height. So, on the plan, mark these details. Then, when you have a balance, begin to write in plant names that match the colours, shapes and sizes you have selected.

In a formal garden, the dividing lines are easy to determine but it is the informal site which is in danger of degenerating to chaos unless you include a selection of architectural plants. You can divide the area into blocks or sections and plan accordingly. If you are fond of colour mixtures do not be afraid to alternate the mixes with groups of single colours or blocks of foliage to consolidate the planting.

Plain blue cornflowers, such as 'Blue Diadem', sown in the autumn with orange calendulas (the old variety 'Radio' is still one of the finest), flower the following summer, but provide a foliage cover meanwhile. In mild conditions, early sown calendula will show a bud or two before winter's end.

Sown in June or July, winter-flowering pansies (strictly speaking these are perennials) will provide a scattering of blooms from autumn right through winter and can be used to break the monotony of a green winter garden. They come in a vast number of shades.

For pretty autumn foliage, two interesting thistles – *Silybum marianum* and *Galactites tomentosa* – have marbled rosettes which elongate in the spring as the plants mature. Both self-seed freely.

For sheer size and character, I would include some annual mallows, not the livid purple *Malva mauritiana* which has crept into vogue lately because it is such a coarse grower, but the clean, pink *Lavatera* 'Silver Cup' and its lovely white counterpart 'Mont Blanc'. Annual sunflowers, by no means things of beauty, are nevertheless important in the annuals garden.

Scent is a vital ingredient and can be provided by sweet peas and mignonette.

Finally, I would sow the seed of *Limnanthes douglasii*. Along the front of the border, at the bases of walls, at the roots of trees or shrubs, under hedges, in fact, anywhere where a little lift of instant colour is warranted.

Half-hardy annuals provide the most rapid display of any garden plants.

1 *Collinsia heterophylla*
2 *Papaver rhoeas* (field poppy)
3 Cornflower
4 *Calendula* (pot marigold)
5 Shirley poppy
6 *Iberis amara* (candytuft)
7 Mignonette
8 *Limnanthes douglasii*
9 Nigella (love-in-a-mist)
10 *Lavatera* 'Silver Cup'
11 Larkspur

AN EXPOSED GARDEN

SHORT CUT RATING ★★

MAINTENANCE At first ★★
then ★★★

ASPECT
Reasonable soil, good drainage
but exposed to all four winds

**Rapid shrubs such as sorbaria
and robus provide a speedy
display while shelter plants get
large enough to protect the rest.
Fast herbaceous plants mat
together to make a weed-proof
ground cover.**

1 *Betula utilis*
2 *Cornus alba* 'Sibirica'
3 *Geranium macrorrhizum*
4 *Sorbaria aitchinsonii*
5 **Dianthus**
6 *Alchemilla mollis*
7 *Geranium endressii*
8 *Centranthus ruber*
9 *Rubus* 'Benenden'
10 *Rosa rugosa*
11 **Ilex standard**
12 *Cryptomeria japonica*

Little will thrive until the wind can be kept off, so the first aim must be to establish sheltering plants (see page 44). Apart from the Leyland cypresses and other hedging plants discussed on pages 60 and 123, shelter belt trees include alder, beech, yew or even Scots pine. All these grow large, however, and are unsuitable for a small garden, unless they are prevented from reaching their natural size by pruning and clipping. Occasional placings of birch add winter interest when their pale trunks show up well against the dark green of the conifers.

In more restricted gardens or on the inside of the tree shelter, plant big evergreen shrubs. Conifers such as *Cryptomeria japonica* and *Chamaecyparis pisifera* do eventually get quite large but they take a long time getting there and as young trees make handsome shelter plants. A group of middle growth rate conifers like these, selected for contrasting colours and habits, make a fine backdrop.

Interim shrubs which will grow in exposed conditions are useful while the main shelter belt is developing. These can be removed later, to make room for something more choice.

Stalwart, windproof shrubs include *Sorbaria aitchisonii* – a great, sprawling plant which suckers freely and produces big, creamy inflorescences in early summer. Similar in its habits is the bramble relative, *Rubus deliciosus*, or, better still, *R.* 'Benenden'. This has long, lax stems smothered with rose-like white flowers, each with its bunch of golden stamens.

For winter delights, a windy garden benefits from a collection of pollarded shrubs. *Cornus alba* is best for this and, in summer, looks well with the rubus or the sorbaria. The form 'Sibirica' has the reddest stems and these look even better planted near two others: 'Kesselringii' which has black bark and dark foliage in summer and *Cornus stolonifera* 'Flaviramea' whose stems are pale olive green. These plants are impervious to wind and not unattractive in summer but in winter, what a trio they make!

The tougher of the shrub roses are weatherproof. Anything with *Rosa rugosa* in its blood is a safe bet so, besides those mentioned on page 122, look for the gorgeous white 'Blanc Double de Coubert' or the stunning wine red 'Mrs Anthony Waterer'. For handsome autumn fruits, the *Rosa moyesii* tribe are best, being windproof and gorgeous looking into the bargain. Besides the species itself, look for the deep pink 'Arthur Hillier' and slightly paler 'Highdownensis'. A great, sprawling, weatherproof shrub rose that has done exceptionally well for me is 'Cerise Bouquet'.

As for herbaceous plants, the low, tough kinds descended from wayside weeds are easily the best. Garden pinks disregard drying winds, flowering all the better for a bit of tough going. Cranesbills, especially *Geranium endressii* and *G. macrorrhizum* are fine in exposed spots, flowering in early summer and having attractive foliage at other times. The wall valerian (*Centranthus ruber*) is utterly indestructible.

A BOG AND WATER GARDEN

Outline plants that will tolerate wet feet include bamboos, most willows, several species of alder, particularly *Alnus glutinosa* whose winter catkins are a delight, and the magnificent swamp cypress (*Taxodium distichum*), a deciduous conifer with fresh, green spring foliage and fine autumn colour.

Among marshland beauties, you will need *Lysichiton americanus*, often mistakenly called skunk cabbage, for its huge yellow spathes in spring followed by handsome foliage. (If you want real skunk cabbage, look for *Symplocarpus foetidus* which also has superb foliage but repulsive flowers which smell like dead stoats.)

The finest wetland fern is the ostrich fern (*Matteuccia struthiopteris*) which emerges like a giant shuttlecock in late spring. Royal fern (*Osmunda regalis*) is another perfect marsh fern which will grow in water or wet ground.

Bog primulas and irises make up the best of the early summer colour. The candelabra primulas from Asia have been improved so that the hybrids are now better garden plants than the original species but have lost none of their simple beauty. The warm coppery red, orange and salmon shades are descended, mainly, from *Primula bulleyana* whereas the pinks, wine reds and whites come from *P. japonica* and *P. pulverulenta*. Many of these have a pale mealiness on their stems, adding greatly to their charms, and all seed freely.

Of irises, the big, floppy Japanese types are the most sensational, particularly *Iris kaempferi*

(now called *I. ensata.*) and *I. laevigata*. These have huge, flattened flowers in gentle pastel shades. Among smaller species, the most bewitching blooms belong to the black form of *I. chrysographes*. The buds are as jet but the open blooms have the slightest hint of midnight purple – which looks glorious when grown with white columbines or the white and green *Astrantia major*.

Later in summer, when the plants have reached a climax of growth, the dark bronze foliage and burning red blooms of *Lobelia fulgens* make a lovely contribution, especially if planted in bold groups, preferably in full sunshine where their colours are even more intense. The foliage of big, thrusting plants like *Rheum palmatum* and tall grasses such as *Miscanthus sinensis* or *Spartina pectinata* make a good contrast in colour and texture.

In late summer, the ligularias, which will have contributed foliage all season, burst into flower and change the mood to one of gold and orange. *Ligularia dentata* 'Desdemona' is one of the finest, with brilliant orange daisy-like flowers and generous, rounded leaves, bottle green above and deep purple beneath.

All the plants mentioned so far grow tall but even a bog has areas where tiny species belong. The delightful bird's eye primrose (*Primula farinosa*) is far too lovely to leave out, with its dainty pink blooms in spring, and looks delightful alongside the double version of the cuckoo flower, *Cardamine pratensis* 'Flore Pleno'.

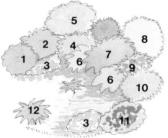

In the wet, foliage is bold and growth speedy. The choice of short-cut plants is, therefore, much wider than in most other garden settings.

1 *Ligularia dentata*
2 *Lysichiton camtschatcensis*
3 *Primula japonica* 'Postford White'
4 *Osmunda regalis*
5 *Alder*
6 *Lysichiton americanus*
7 *Rheum palmatum*
8 *Salix exigua*
9 *Iris laevigata*
10 *Matteuccia struthiopteris*
11 *Primula pulverulenta*
12 *Iris kaempferi*

A CONTAINER GARDEN

SHORT CUT RATING ★★★

MAINTENANCE ★ to **★★★**
Summer ★★★
Winter ★
Single Plants ★

Groups of containers can be assembled in a matter of moments to compose an instant garden.

1 Houseleek
2 *Helichrysum petiolare* and pink trailing pelargonium
3 *Eucalyptus gunnii*
4 Sempervivum
5 Echeveria
6 Variegated trailing pelargonium
7 Fuchsia
8 *Pelargonium* 'L'Elégante'

The quickest instant garden of all is a container garden. With a little imagination, a strong back and a fat wallet, you could visit a garden centre in a morning and transform your bare site into a garden that afternoon! But container gardens can be built almost anywhere within a garden and out of very little.

Since containers provide the biggest single – and in some cases the only – opportunity for short-cut gardening, they should always be high on your list of possibilities. In addition to the several different containers discussed here, other container recipes to consider include herb gardens, which look attractive and provide something useful for the kitchen, sinks or troughs for alpines, or even water tubs planted with aquatics and stocked with fish! Almost every known plant will tolerate life in a container and a great many actually prefer being potted (page 128).

SUMMER POTS

Instant they are but not exactly maintenance-free. Summer plants such as fuchsias, petunias, impatiens and so on all need regular feeding and constant watering. But, provided the containers are well designed, free-draining and provide plenty of room for root development, regular maintenance is by no means arduous – and can be enjoyable. Automatic watering

systems makes things even simpler and are invaluable when you go on holiday.

The best summer plants for pots are those that flower profusely all season or, at least, have attractive foliage. Keeping the colour scheme simple makes a planting more effective so, instead of going for mixtures, consider using just one or, at the most, two colours. White, even on its own, makes a delightful base colour with which to contrast foliage either in deep green or, for a gentler display, silver. Thus, a summer container planted with white pelargoniums or petunias could be backed up with the ubiquitous, silver-foliaged *Helichrysum petiolare*, with a white standard fuchsia, perhaps, or with the glaucous foliage of a young seedling of *Eucalyptus gunnii*.

In total contrast, a hot theme might be based around the red-leaved castor oil plant, *Ricinus communis* 'Impala'. The glowing red dahlia 'Bishop of Llandaff' makes a fine companion for this because its foliage is dark and bronzy. To brighten the whole, a shock of silver or cream foliage would be effective but it might be more dramatic to maintain the dark foliage and hot flower theme by planting *Lobelia cardinalis* opposite the dahlia and by trailing the scarlet *Verbena peruviana* over the sides. Then, the container would look almost as though it were on fire.

Such themes can be replicated in any

number of colour combinations. The great thing is to be daring and experimental. If you hate it, re-plant. What have you to lose?

For low maintenance, summer containers can be planted with slower growing plants. Echeverias can be effective, coming as they do, in such an interesting number of forms with so many different leaf and flower colours. On a smaller scale, I enjoy houseleeks (sempervivums and jovibarbas) because they are pretty well drought proof and quietly exist without demanding much attention. There are several named varieties with varying rosette colours from rich mahogany red to emerald green that look good when massed together.

A WINTER TUB

Permanent plantings in containers can have as much charm as bright, summer flowers, and in winter there need never be a shortage of interest from plants of all shapes and sizes. Such plantings are especially useful near doors.

Try a foliage and flower combination with heathers, perhaps in varieties such as the soft pink 'Darley Dale' or the pure white 'Ada S. Collings'. Their tufty foliage will contrast with the bold leaves of *Bergenia* 'Abendglut' or the species *B. purpurascens* which turns bronze in cold weather. They will flower at winter's end and continue to bloom well into spring.

Ivy, especially the small-leaved kinds like *Hedera helix* 'Marmorata Minor', helps to complete the ensemble, but you will need a clump or two of snowdrops or other winter-flowering bulbs for extra flower power. Dubbed vulgar by some, the big Dutch crocuses are great favourites of mine and in a collection of sombre, evergreen plants, the large white flowers of *Crocus* 'Jeanne d'Arc' are breath-taking, especially when they open to the sun.

SINGLE PLANTS

As well as compositions, do not overlook the great value of a single plant in a container. The eighteenth century gardeners knew what they were about when they set up ranks of orange plants in wooden tubs on their stately parterres. A single evergreen, or perhaps a pair, clipped to a specific shape, brings instant life and not a little architecture to a new garden. A tree in a tub, for example, could make the centre point of a roof or balcony garden.

Buying mature potted evergreens, ready clipped, can be very expensive but it is not difficult to do your own topiary, starting with unclipped specimens. It does take time to get them into their ultimate desired shape, but at least they will be contributing something to your short-cut garden as soon as you introduce them, and can be most rewarding.

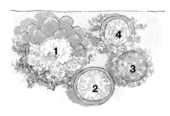

Although there is less choice than in summer, a group of winter containers can give a lasting show of greenery with splashes of colour throughout the dark months.

1 *Crocus* **'Jeanne d'Arc', bergenia,** *Lamium maculatum* **'Beacon Silver',** *Hedera helix* **'Atropurpurea'**

2 **Snowdrop**

3 *Erica erigena* **'Irish Dusk'**

4 **Muscari and** *Hedera helix* **'Glacier'**

A WILD GARDEN

SHORT CUT RATING ★★

MAINTENANCE ★★

ASPECT
Sun to semi-shade, on neutral soil
which is free-draining but not rich

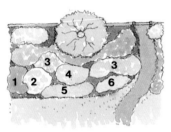

**An old tree makes a starting
point for a new wild garden.
Rapid colonizers have been
blended with species that
develop more sedately.**
1 **Epimedium**
2 **Cowslip**
3 **Wild daffodil**
4 **Trillium**
5 **Snowdrop and crocus**
6 *Geranium phaeum*

A wild garden can easily incorporate a small grassy flower meadow, where a mixture of grasses and wildflowers co-habit. Pathways, meandering through the meadow section and leading to a focal point, a seat under the tree perhaps, are easily made and maintained as close-mown grass.

The boundary between the more disciplined part of a garden and the wild zone can be maintained simply by mowing up to the long grass. Under trees, the wild area boundary follows the 'drip line' – that is, the outer limits of a tree's branches where most of the rain drips onto the ground. Incidentally, it is around the drip line that you are likely to find the greatest concentration of active tree roots and, because of the competition they provide, an almost natural boundary will occur there.

During winter and early spring, the areas under deciduous trees are well lit but in summer they are quite heavily shaded. And since trees absorb a great deal of water from the ground, the soil immediately beneath the branches tends to become dry in summer. But the shade keeps it cool and, as the plants which grow in those dull conditions do little more than tick over during high summer, this poses no serious problem. Woodland plants grow where there is plenty of leaf litter. In some habitats this may be several centimetres thick, gradually rotting down at the lowest level and becoming incorporated, thanks to the activities of earthworms, into the topsoil. Such organic material

provides little in the way of plant nutrients, indeed, it can have the effect of locking away nitrogen, but it does enhance the physical condition of the soil, improving its ability to retain moisture and keeping the roots of the plants cool.

Ponds are also excellent short-cut features that particularly suit a wild garden, bringing additional planting opportunities; they are discussed in detail on pages 95–103.

As well as periods of glory, all wild gardens have untidy spells. Late autumn is the season of dying foliage and collapsing stems which look gaunt and forbidding until they have been cleared away, or have rotted down in the winter wet. Under trees, early summer is often disappointing after the colourful carpets of spring bulbs and other plants which love dappled shade. For all but the most fastidious gardeners, these periods are a small price to pay for the peaks of the year but, if you take serious exception to untidy, dying vegetation, perhaps you should consider carefully whether a truly wild garden is really for you.

PLANTING THE WILD GARDEN

The most popular winter flowers in Europe are, surely, winter aconites (*Eranthis*) and snowdrops (*Galanthus*). Where they are happy, they spread every year until they have formed huge drifts of golden yellow and pure white. Their scent, faint outdoors but strong enough for a dozen blooms to perfume a whole living room when picked and brought in, is sweeter than honey. Hellebores, especially the dazzling white *Helleborus niger*, make perfect wild garden plants and can be followed with the green-flowered stinking hellebore (*Helleborus foetidus*) and wine-red, pale pink and greenish white shades of the *Helleborus orientalis* hybrids.

Spring is the natural season for wild gardens. Just think of the spring flowers in the woodlands of the world! In North America, wakerobin (*Trillium grandiflorum*) carpets the woodland floors, in Britain, bluebells make a sweet-scented, azure haze at about the same time of year. Europe boasts oxlips, with their nodding, butter-coloured flowers and in northern China or Korea, there might be carpetings of brightly coloured azaleas or drifts of Asiatic primulas.

All these plants can be grown together in the wild garden. Because they all enjoy the same habitat, they do not look out of place together, even though they come from different corners of the world. A low-growing combination of crocuses, primroses, wild daffodils, wood anemones, snake's head fritillaries, and violets makes a carpet of jewel-like flowers which is self-perpetuating and requires very little management.

Even if there is insufficient room for a whole wild garden, a planting of this kind is perfect under a lawn tree or in a quiet, shady corner. The added advantage is that grass mowing, usually difficult in such places, need only happen three or four times in late summer and autumn.

In the open meadow section, wild narcissus species will look attractive with scillas but the most beloved meadow flower of all Europe must surely be the cowslip. If happy, it will multiply from seed and, over the years, develop a thriving colony. With pasque flowers (*Pulsatilla vulgaris*), salad burnet (*Sanguisorba minor*) and, in damper soils, bugle (*Ajuga reptans*) and water avens (*Geum rivale*) you have the makings of a delightful spring meadow.

In summer, the shade thrown by the emerging leaves of trees slows things down but there can be some fine displays of foliage underneath it at this time of year. Most members of the forget-me-not family have interesting late foliage. The lungworts (*Pulmonaria*) and *Brunnera macrophylla* are good examples. False

spikenard, *Smilacina racemosa* and the related Solomon's seal (*Polygonatum multiflorum*) make a cool, leafy ground cover after flowering.

Among lilies, the Turk's cap (*Lilium martagon*) enjoys shade which is not too dry and, if the soil is damp and leafy, the North American *Lilium pardalinum* will provide a startling display of spotted scarlet, orange and yellow blooms.

While the shady section goes into eclipse, the meadow reaches a growth climax with all the typical hayfield flowers of knapweed (*Centaurea scabiosa* and *C. nigra*), field scabious (*Knautia arvensis*), ox-eye daisies (*Leucanthemum vulgare*), and meadow cranesbills (*Geranium pratense*). These are all of European origin but American prairie plants like bergamot (*Monarda didyma*) or *Echinacea purpurea* will do equally well in a meadow, as will Caucasian favourites of the herbaceous border such as the globe thistle (*Echinops ritro*).

With the arrival of autumn, the meadow slips into decline, but the tree bases are enlivened with autumn-flowering crocuses, colchicums and the exquisite wild cyclamen. Once you have become attached to these, the florist's pot cyclamen will seem coarse and charmless. The hardiest species are *Cyclamen hederifolium* and *C. coum*. The latter flowers from the shortest day onwards – a delight in the heart of winter – but even when not in flower, the marbled foliage of both is a joy.

THE RIGHT BALANCE

Success with the wild garden depends entirely on balance. A balanced ecology where no single species is threatening the rest, takes many years, even centuries to develop in the wild. In a garden, we aim to achieve balance of a sort within a couple of seasons!

The only way to do this is to police the whole area assiduously. Rampaging species must be limited but slow starters need to be encouraged by removing all competition from them while they develop their populations. Every habitat is different and what works well in one garden could fail in another. In general, however, it is worth getting to know which native plants thrive in your area, and which are dangerously invasive. Avoid the latter and plant everything with great caution until you know how it will behave in the artificial situation and conditions of your wild garden.

9

A GARDENER'S GUIDE TO SHORT-CUT PLANTS

A great many plants have been mentioned in the preceding chapters, most of them with reference to specific functions in the short-cut garden. This chapter describes a selection of fast-growing plants for a variety of different uses. The list is not comprehensive as is too little space to mention more. For easy reference the plants are divided into groups according to their garden uses rather than on a purely botanical basis. The groups are: outline shrubs and trees — woody plants with architectural qualities; bulky shrubs for filling spaces; plants for focal points; hedge plants; ground cover plants; taller perennials; climbers and wall plants; plants especially good for containers; water plants.

Short-cut plants include a great many perennials, biennials such as foxgloves and, of course, speedy annuals such as ornamental poppies.

Short-cut ratings are given for most plants.

★★★ Extra fast – bears results within a season

★★ Moderately fast – some results in the second season

★ Not especially fast – but still a good short-cut plant

Catalpa bignonioides

Acer micranthum *is one of the maples grown for its foliage.*

OUTLINE TREES AND SHRUBS

Acer ★
Maple

Shapely trees and shrubs with handsome foliage and good colour, especially in autumn. The majority are shade tolerant but few, apart from *A. platanoides*, enjoy life in an exposed spot. Fine examples, in decreasing order of size, are *A. platanoides* 'Crimson King', purple foliage; *A. p.* 'Drummondii', variegated; *A. rubrum* 'Scanlon', erect shape, excellent autumn colour and fine foliage but not suitable for shallow, chalky soils; *A. japonicum* 'Vitifolium', slow growing, but superb in colour, right from its early days, with wine-red leaves in autumn.

Aesculus ★★★
Buckeye, horse chestnut

Easy, fast-growing trees and shrubs. *A. hippocastanum* (common horse chestnut) is too large for a small garden, but achieves mature status quite quickly. It has white blossoms in late spring, and fine autumn colour from the palmate foliage. *A. indica* (Indian chestnut), elegant even in its sapling stages, is smaller and more refined with glossy foliage and white flowers in summer. *A. parviflora* is a suckering shrub with pretty white flowers.

Ailanthus altissima ★★★
Tree of Heaven

Rapid, suckering tree with graceful foliage. If cut to the ground every season, it produces a vigorous forest of stems with much larger foliage than on the mature tree, useful in small gardens.

Betula ★★
Birch

Medium to rapid trees, beautiful because of their pale, papery bark and graceful forms. Worthwhile birches include *B. jacquemontii* for its snow-white trunk, yellow autumn foliage and rapid growth; *B. pendula* (European silver birch) and *B. utilis* whose trunks are buff and papery.

Catalpa bignonioides ★★★
Indian bean tree

Rapid growth, generous spreading proportions and huge leaves. The midsummer white flowers are a worthwhile bonus.

Cedrus ★
Cedar

Not especially fast but superbly shaped trees, perfect for a good outline. Not water dependent, but they grow better in rich, moist soil. Good species include *C. deodara* (deodar) and *C. atlantica* (Atlas cedar).

Crataegus ★★★
Thorn

Rapid trees with good shape and character, tolerant of exposed positions and poor soil. Fastest species include garden forms of *C. oxyacantha*, such as the red double 'Paul's Scarlet'. *C. prunifolia* is excellent for autumn colour and the smaller, slower but shapely *C. tanacetifolia* has a distinctive character and fine winter outline.

Eucalyptus ★★★
Gum

Hundred of species, most of which grow into large, good-natured trees, putting up with exposed positions and poor soil but not able to survive cold winters. They respond to hard pruning, often producing immature foliage which differs from the mature. The two most dependable species for colder areas are *E. gunnii* and, for smaller gardens, *E. niphophila* (snow gum).

Ilex
Holly

Not short-cut plants but as they are attractive from a very early age and have many uses, hollies will always find a place in the well-husbanded garden. Certain varieties, such as *I. × altaclarensis* 'Belgica Aurea' and *I. aquifolium* 'Pyramidalis' are especially shapely and grow faster than average hollies.

Malus ★★
Apple
🗲❀❊

Useful genus of flowering trees. Ornamental kinds for short-cut gardeners include the edible crab *M.* 'John Downie' for fruit, *M.* 'Profusion' or *M.* 'Hillieri' for blossoms and *M. tschonoskii* for autumn colour.

Parrotia persica ★★★
♠🗲🌿❀❊

Rapid, spreading trees with superb autumn colour. Can be trained on a framework to create early structure.

Prunus ★–★★★
🗲 or ♠🗲❀❊

Huge genus of garden shrubs and trees. Especially fast are: *P.* 'Amanogawa', erect habit; *P.* 'Tai-haku', huge, white flowers; *P.* × *subhirtella ascendens* 'Autumnalis', winter flowers; *P. dulcis* (almond), early blossom; *P. sargentii*, red autumn colour and deep pink blossom.

Salix ★★★
Willow
🗲❀≋●❊

Fast trees and shrubs, many with good architectural qualities and outstanding winter interest. Larger species can be pollarded – cut hard back and made to produce young stems each season. Useful willows, in decreasing order of size, include: *S. matsudana* 'Tortuosa', twisted twigs for a fine winter background; *S. alba* 'Sericea', silver foliage; *S. daphnoides*, fine catkins; *S. purpurea* 'Pendula', small leaves, reddish stems, weeping branches; and *S. fargesii*, dark reddish, polished winter twigs, handsome summer foliage.

Sorbus aria and relatives ★★★
Whitebeam
♠🗲🌿❀❊

Invaluable short-cut trees which have fine shapes in their youth and grow quickly to maturity. Many are suitable for small gardens. Notable kinds include: *S. aria* 'Lutescens' whose leaves emerge from silver buds; *S. a.* 'Mitchellii', huge foliage; and the lovely *S. intermedia* (Swedish whitebeam), lobed leaves and red berries.

Sorbus aucuparia and relatives ★★★
Rowan
♠🗲❀🌿❊

Elegant foliage, fine blossoms, beautiful berries and pleasing shapes. These ideal trees seldom grow large enough to be troublesome. *S. aucuparia* 'Rossica', superb red berries; *S. cashmiriana*, white berries, pink blossoms; and *S.* 'Apricot Lady', semi-erect habit, amber fruits.

BULKY SHRUBS

Aralia elata ★★
Angelica tree
♠🗲❀🌿❊☀❅

Stubby, suckering shrubs with enormous compound leaves and creamy white flowers. Ideal for fast foliage.

Bamboos ★★★
♠♣🗲≋●☀❊

Plants which form thickets of wands, covered with rustling, evergreen foliage. Some, like *Sinarundinaria anceps* and clump-forming, apple-green leaved *Arundinaria murielae* (syn. *Thamnocalamus spathaceus*) grow tall quite quickly, especially in moist soil. Dwarf species include *Pleioblastus auricomus* whose leaves are striped olive, lime green and gold.

Buddleia davidii ★★★
Butterfly bush
🗲❀❊☀

Rapid shrubs with fragrant midsummer flowers in purple shades. Best cut back each spring but, if left, will grow into large screening plants up to 5m/15ft high in a couple of seasons. Good cultivars include the blue-mauve flowered *B. d.* 'Lochinch', silvery foliage; *B. d.* 'Black Knight', deep purple; *B. d.* 'Royal Red', magenta rather than red; *B. d.* 'Pink Delight'; and *B. d.* 'White Cloud'.

Cornus alba and relatives ★★
Dogwood
🗲🌿☀❊

Useful for their red or green winter twigs and quick to fill their space (2m/6ft). Among the best for summer foliage are *C. a.* 'Elegantissima', *C. a.* 'Spaethii', both of which are variegated, and *C. a.* 'Aurea' whose gold foliage turns rusty in autumn.

Cornus mas ★★
Cornelian cherry
♠🗲❀🌿≋❊

Shapely shrub growing to 3m/10ft or more, with spreading branches, small, star-shaped, yellow winter blossom and fine, dark green foliage colouring well in autumn.

Corylus avellana ★★★
Hazel, cobnut
🗲❀🌿≋●❊

Soft foliage on quick-growing wands which branch in their second year. Fine catkins in late winter and edible nuts. Look for purple-leaved *C. a.* 'Purpurea'. There is also a gold-leaved form and one with twisted branches, *C. a.* 'Contorta', useful for winter outline.

Whitebeam

Short-cut ratings are given for most plants.

★★★ Extra fast – bears results within a season

★★ Moderately fast – some results in the second season

★ Not especially fast – but still a good short-cut plant

Cotinus coggygria ★★
Smoke bush

Shapely, bushy plants with glorious foliage, good autumn colour and hazy seedheads. *C. g.* 'Royal Purple' has the darkest leaves but the hybrid, *C. g.* 'Grace', has the finest leaves which turn a beautiful wine red in autumn.

Garrya elliptica ★

Not as fast as some shrubs, but a worthy evergreen which looks mature when young and flowers with elegant, light green catkins from mid-winter to early spring. Grows to about 2.3m/7ft when set against a wall.

Hydrangea macrophylla ★★★
Hortensia

Mophead hydrangeas bulk up fast and flower profusely. Though hardy and lime tolerant, they dislike thin, chalky soils and tend to lose flower buds in extreme frost.

Leycesteria formosa ★★★
Himalayan honeysuckle

Rapid thicket former, to 2m/6ft, with graceful flowers which hang, catkin-like, in wine red tassels.

Philadelphus ★★★
Mock Orange

Medium to large, shrubs with fragrant white or cream flowers in late spring. *P. coronarius* is best for small gardens but varieties like *P.* 'Belle Etoile' or *P.* 'Beauclerk' make a more dramatic gesture quickly. Mock oranges thrive in the poorest soils. Cut back some of the older shoots to young growth after flowering.

Piptanthus laburnifolius ★★

Evergreen member of the pea family with palmate leaves, very green stems and bright yellow flowers in spring. Grows to 2m/6ft, or more when against a warm wall. (Syn. *Piptanthus nepalensis*)

Rhododendron ★

The most vigorous for rapid growth include the invasive *R. ponticum* (3m/10ft) but dwarf varieties are also good short-cut plants because they are shapely at an early age and contribute colour and evergreen foliage. The *R. yakushimanum* hybrids are deservedly popular.

Rosa

Roses are the most popular and versatile genus in the garden. Short-cut roses need to provide spectacle quickly. To do this, they need vigour, beauty and height. Fragrance, good autumn foliage and attractive fruits are also important considerations. There are so many that to list only a few seems like discriminating against the majority. In addition to the ones mentioned below, 'Frühlingsmorgen' and 'Frühlingsgold' are both speedy, as are the scented leaved 'Meg Merrilees' and 'Complicata'.

Rosa moyesii and hybrids ★★★

Large shrubs to 2.6m/8ft or more with single flowers and large hips. Look for red 'Geranium' and pink 'Highdownensis'. A close relative, is 'Nevada', semi-double pinkish white, and its pink sport, 'Marguerite Hilling'.

Rosa rugosa ★★★

Disease-resistant, stocky plants with fragrant blossom, good hips and an upright habit. Look for 'Roseraie de l'Haÿ', purple red; 'Blanc Double de Coubert', white; and 'Agnes', primrose yellow.

Rosa spinosissima ★★★
Scotch briar, Burnet rose

Suckering plants with bristling stems usually growing to about 1m/3ft or more, and small but showy flowers. 'Dunwich', cream; 'William III', pink; and 'Glory of Edzell', salmon. All have a sweet scent. Useful historic roses include 'Charles de Mills', 'Fantin Latour' and *R. alba* 'Maxima'.

Sambucus ★★★
Elder

Two main species, *S. nigra* and *S. racemosa* are both quick to establish and grow to 2.6/8ft or more, even in adverse conditions. Several garden forms are especially valuable including *S. n.* 'Guincho Purple', *S. n.* 'Aurea' and the cut-leaved *S. n. laciniata*. The most popular form of *S. racemosa* is 'Plumosa Aurea'.

Viburnum ★★

A large and valuable genus of shrubs, many with fragrant flowers. Evergreen: *V. tinus*, *V. rhytidophyllum* and *V. davidii*. Deciduous: *V. farreri*, *V. × bodnantense* (both winter flowering), *V. carlesii* 'Diana', *V. opulus* 'Sterile' and *V. plicatum*. Two rarer species of great charm are the slightly tender *V. odoratissimum*, whose evergreen foliage has a silicon gloss, and the lanky *V. nudum*.

Cotinus coggygria

PLANTS FOR FOCAL POINTS

Acanthus spinosus ★★

Vigorous shocks of lobed and toothed foliage emerge in spring followed by dramatic 1.3m/4ft flower spikes in green, pink and white.

Cornus controversa

Not a short-cut plant but so valuable, with its tiered branches, as a centrepiece.

Crambe cordifolia ★★★

Giant member of the cabbage family. Deep green foliage above which tower 2m/6ft, much-branched flower stems carrying hundreds of tiny white blooms.

Euphorbia characias ★★★

Shrubby evergreens with stiff stems and greenish flowers from late winter to early summer. The subspecies *E. c. wulfenii* is especially good because of the golden tinge to its flowers.

Fritillaria imperialis ★★★

Crown imperial

Dramatic bulbous plant which shoots up to 1m/3ft within a few days and flowers with nodding orange or yellow bells.

Rheum palmatum ★★★

Giant rhubarb foliage. Plants reach a metre across within a season.

Verbascum bombyciferum ★★★

A giant mullein with silver meal on the foliage and 2.6m/8ft spikes of acid-yellow flowers in summer. Biennial but a free seeder.

Yucca gloriosa ★

Spiky, evergreen foliage with huge spires of waxy cream to white flowers in summer.

HEDGE PLANTS

Carpinus betula ★

Hornbeam

A fine hedge, especially for heavy soils. The bright green foliage turns beige and persists through winter. A single annual clip will suffice to keep it looking good.

Crataegus monogyna ★★

Hawthorn

Loses its winter foliage but is graced in spring with white blossom which gives rise to red berries (haws) in the autumn. A wildlife-friendly plant, only suitable for an informal, rural-style hedge.

× Cupressocyparis leylandii ★★★

Leyland cypress

One of the fastest growing hybrid conifers. In the right place, and in the right hands, it can be trained into a perfect formal hedge within three seasons. It is relatively hardy and comes in several attractive clones offering subtle variations in foliage colour and habit. × C. l. 'Castlewellan', has a yellowish caste and × C. l. 'Harlequin' is deep green with cream flecks among the young foliage.

Cupressus macrocarpa ★★

Monterey cypress

One of the parents of Leyland cypress but considerably less coarse, with pleasantly aromatic foliage. Although not hardy in excessively cold climates, it clips into a perfect evergreen hedge. The variety *C. m.* 'Goldcrest' is emerald green.

Elaeagnus × ebbingei ★★

A fine evergreen with rufous stems, rusty undersides to the shiny green leaves and small but intensely fragrant blossoms in late summer.

Fagus sylvatica ★

Beech

Some of the finest hedges in the world are beech. In good conditions it is faster than you might expect but on an exposed site, in poor soil, it seems to take forever, but is worth the wait. *F. s. purpurea*, (purple beech) is attractive.

Ligustrum ovalifolium ★★

Privet

Well-known evergreen which grows fast enough to need several clips through the summer. Rather dull and prone to honey fungus but still a good hedge plant, especially to hide behind.

Prunus laurocerasus ★★

Cherry laurel

One of the fastest broad-leaved evergreens. Dark, glossy foliage and, sometimes, white flowers followed by black berries. Responds well to feeding, growing at twice the rate in fertile soil.

KEY

◢ Acid or neutral soil only – lime haters

♠ Architectural quality – outstanding shapes

∅ Deciduous – loses leaves in winter

♠ Evergreen

✿ Flowers (or fruits) – prized for blooming quality

🍃 Foliage – prized for leaves

▨ Drought tolerant

≋ Moisture-loving plants – not necessarily aquatics

● Shade-loving plants

☀ Sun-loving plants

✳ Tender in cold areas – barely frost hardy

❅ Plants which have some winter interest

Euphorbia characias

Short-cut ratings are given for most plants.

★★★ Extra fast – bears results within a season

★★ Moderately fast – some results in the second season

★ Not especially fast – but still a good short-cut plant

Alchemilla

Freely seeding foxgloves are useful short-cut plants.

GROUND COVER PLANTS

Alchemilla ★★★
Lady's mantle

Herbaceous members of the rose family with sprays of tiny yellow-green flowers and attractive foliage. *A. mollis* is the largest, growing to about 45cm/18in, with rounded leaves, but the smaller *A. conjuncta*, 15cm/6in, is equally pretty, with silver-backed leaves and musk-scented flowers.

Astrantia ★★★
Masterwort

Easy plants which colonize well by seeding and spreading. The flowers are greenish or pinkish, distinctively crown shaped. It pays to select seed from good plants to improve the strain you grow. Good garden forms include *A. major rubra*, *A. m.* 'Shaggy' and the species *A. maxima*.

Bergenia cordifolia and relatives ★★★

Leathery, evergreen foliage, forming thick, weed-proof layers. Flowers emerge in late winter and spring and are varying shades of pink or white. Several varieties have leaves which turn bronze in cold weather. Look for white *B.* 'Silberlicht', pink *B.* 'Bressingham Salmon' and *B.* 'Abendglut' – intense cerise with good leaf colour.

Centranthus ruber ★★★
Red valerian

A common but underrated perennial which grows to 1m/3ft in any soil, even the poorest, as long as it is in full light. There are brick red, pinkish red and white forms.

Geranium ★★★
Cranesbill
or

Quick, easy perennials with attractive foliage and delicate flowers in blue, pink, or shades in between. Low, spreading cranesbills include *G. sanguineum*, *G. himalayense* and various hybrids including *G.* 'Claridge Druce', *G.* 'Russel Pritchard' and *G.* × *cantabrigiense*.

Geranium macrorrhizum ★★★

Worthy of its own entry, this is arguably the finest all-round ground cover plant in cultivation. The foliage is aromatic, produced in weed-smothering quantities and colours up well in autumn. The early summer pink flowers are all the more beautiful for their dark stamens and graceful carriage. It seems able to survive anywhere.

Lamium maculatum ★★★
Dead-nettle

Invasive plants but beautiful for much of the year and invaluable for filling space quickly. The foliage is striped with silver, and flowers range in colour from deep plum pink to pure white. *L. galeobdolon* is an even more invasive dead-nettle with silver markings and a creeping habit.

Pulmonaria ★★★
Lungwort

The distinctive foliage of these shade-loving plants makes them a worthy choice for ground cover. The three main species grown are *P. saccharata*, *P. rubra* and *P. angustifolia*. The spring flowers vary from deep blue through mauve to pink or white. Foliage in many is attractively stippled or blotched with silver.

Stachys byzantina ★★★
Lamb's ears

Woolly, silvery foliage and thickly carpeting habit, especially good for dry conditions. There are several fine garden forms including *S. b.* 'Silver Carpet' and a gold-leaved variety called *S. b.* 'Primrose Heron'.

Symphytum ★★★
Comfrey

Rather coarse perennials but many have good foliage and they all have vigour. Good garden sorts include the dwarf, but creeping, *S. grandiflorum* 'Variegatum' and the taller *S. uplandicum* 'Variegatum' whose foliage has bold, cream markings. Subject to rust in dry conditions.

TALLER PERENNIALS

Anemone ★★
Windflower

⊛ ☀

Most windflowers are low growing but the stately *A. japonica* reaches a metre, with large flowers in shades of pink or white. Excellent for dry soil.

Aquilegia ★★★
Columbine

⊛ ✦ ● ☀

Fast, long lasting and free seeding. Distinctively shaped flowers are held well above decorative foliage. Best planted in drifts where they make plenty of colour in late spring.

Aster ★★★
Michaelmas daisy

⊛ ✦

A variable genus, the majority of species flowering after the longest day. Rapid developers include: disease-resistant *A. novae-angliae*; *A. ×frikartii*, because of its large yellow-centred blue flowers produced over long periods; and the lower growing *A. ericoides*, which produces a mist of tiny flowers every autumn.

Campanula ★★★
Bellflower

♠ ⊛ ● ☀

Bell-shaped flowers in all sizes and a feast of cool coloration from pure white, through the blues to pinkish mauve. The largest, *C. lactiflora* and *C. latifolia*, grow to 1.6m/5ft and are positively architectural but mid-sized species, such as *C. latiloba* and *C. takesimana*, are equally dramatic.

Carex ★★★
Sedge

♠ ✦ ≋ ●

Grass-like plants, many of great beauty. Being fast, easy and of good architectural value, they are the archetypal short-cut plant. Species of especial value include *C. pendula*, for its shocks of foliage and tall, graceful flowers, and *C. buchananii*, for its interesting, rusty leaves.

Dendranthema ★★★
Florists' chrysanthemum

⊛ ☀ ❋

Bright flowers in a warm colour range, blooming from the end of summer until early winter. The hardiest and most perennial types include Korean 'chrysanthemums' which have sprays of small flowers and the formerly named *Chrysanthemum rubellum* varieties, such as 'Clara Curtis'. (Recent re-naming of this genus has caused much confusion among gardeners.)

Digitalis ★★★
Foxglove

♠ ⊛ ✦ ● ☀

Small but choice group of plants, mainly biennials, with tall flower spikes and tube-shaped flowers. *D. purpurea*, (common foxglove), is the most decorative, with blooms ranging in colour from purple to pink or white but *D. ferruginea* has intriguing flowers marked with rust and cream.

Grasses ★★★
♠ ⊛ ✦ ≋ ● ☀ ❋ ✄

Most garden grasses are good short-cut plants, from huge pampas grasses, such as *Cortaderia selloana*, to more modest species like blue fescue or the graceful *Helictotrichon sempervirens*. Some are invasive.

Hemerocallis ★★★
Day lily

♠ ● ⊛ ≋ ☀

A huge group of vigorous plants with generous, grassy foliage and flowers in shades of yellow, orange, mahogany and even flesh tones. They will colonize large areas quickly.

Hosta ★
Plantain lily

♠ ✦ ≋ ●

Broad, decorative foliage in every imaginable shade of green. Several species and literally hundreds of named varieties fall into three main colour categories: green, gold and variegated.

Iris ★★
♠ ⊛ ≋ ● ☀ ✄

Good plants for every garden, not just for the fine flowers but also for the sword-like foliage. Bearded irises make a fairly quick display in dry soil. In moist conditions, hybrids of *I. sibirica* are a better choice. Many species flower in winter.

Ligularia ★★★
♠ ⊛ ✦ ≋ ● ☀

Members of the daisy family with dramatic foliage and, usually, orange or yellow flowers. *L. dentata* has big, rounded leaves with dark backs; the variety *L. d.* 'Desdemona' has orange flowers. *L. przewalskii* 'The Rocket' has finer, spoon-shaped, serrated foliage, spidery yellow flowers and a black caste to the stem. Will reach 1.3m/4ft in moist soil.

Lychnis ★★★
Campion

⊛ ✦ ≋ ● ☀

L. coronaria (rose campion) has silver foliage, wine red flowers and is drought proof. For moist conditions, blood red *L. chalcedonica* is fine.

Dendranthema

Short-cut ratings are given
for most plants.

★★★ Extra fast – bears
results within a season

★★ Moderately fast –
some results in the
second season

★ Not especially fast –
but still a good short-
cut plant

Penstemon

The huge, white flowers of
Clematis 'Marie Boisselot'
brighten up a tree.

Macleaya ★★★
Plume Poppy

Rampant, invasive relative of the poppy, ideal for
filling a large area quickly, especially in partial
shade. The hazy, rust-coloured flower spikes may
grow to 2m/6ft or more.

Penstemon ★★★

Most of the herbaceous species and hybrids flower
all summer and come in a wide colour range
including pinks, reds, blues, purple and white.
Hardiness varies but they are all easy to propagate
from cuttings and many seed prolifically.

Rodgersia ★

Huge leaves which grow straight out of the
ground, cream or pink flowers in summer.
Susceptible to wind damage. The best garden
species include *R. pinnata*, with palmate leaves
and pinkish flowers and *R. tabularis* whose leaves
are umbrella shaped.

Rudbeckia ★★
Cone flower

Bright autumn colour from these bold daisy
flowers. Colours range through yellow to orange
or even tan, but the flower centres usually make a
dark contrast. *R. fulgida deamii* is one of the
longest in flower and *R. nitida* 'Goldquelle' is a
double which lacks the dark centres.

CLIMBERS AND WALL PLANTS

Actinidia ★★

Vigorous genus which includes *A. chinensis* (kiwi
fruit). *A. kolomikta* develops pink or white
splashes on its foliage if grown in full sunlight.

Akebia ★★★

Rampant evergreen or semi-evergreen climbers
with curious flowers. *A. quinata* has brownish red
flowers followed by sausage-shaped fruits. *A.
trifoliata* has dark purple flowers. Both will climb
to 10m/30ft or more.

Chaenomeles ★

Hardy shrubs which flower in winter, especially
when grown against a wall. Colours range from
the crimson of *C.* 'Crimson and Gold' through
pinks in varieties such as *C.* 'Pink Lady' and *C.*
'Apple Blossom' to the pure white of *C. speciosa*
'Nivalis'. Excellent frame plants to accommodate
summer climbers such as herbaceous clematis.

Clematis ★★★

SPRING FLOWERING The most vigorous are *C.
montana*, white, and its relatives which all grow
happily in most positions. Good choices include *C.
chrysocoma*, pink, and *C. montana* 'Elizabeth',
pale pink. More restrained in their habits are *C.
alpina* and *C. macropetala*, good examples being
C. a. 'Frances Rivis', blue, nodding flowers, and *C.
m.* 'Markham's Pink'. The toughest evergreen
clematis for spring use is *C. armandii* whose white
flowers are sweetly scented.
SUMMER FLOWERING Most of the large-flowered
hybrids flower at this time. Blues, mauves and
pinks predominate. Early flowering hybrids
include the double blue *C.* 'Countess of Lovelace'
and the pure white *C.* 'Marie Boisselot'. Later
flowering species include *C. viticella* – ideal for
growing into other shrubs because it can be cut
hard back each winter. Yellow Himalayan species
are useful for their fluffy seed heads as well as
their odd-textured flowers. Of these, *C. orientalis*
is the most vigorous but *C. tangutica*, with its
lantern-like blooms, has the edge for beauty.

Clematis ★

WINTER FLOWERING In sheltered regions, one or
two species will flower in winter. *C. cirrhosa
balearica* has flowers the colour of parchment
with little red flecks. The variety *C. c.* 'Freckles'
has blood red blotches. *C. paniculata* is evergreen
with white flowers but is tender.

Eccremocarpus scaber ★★★

Freely seeding herbaceous climbers. The tubular red, orange or yellow flowers, produced all summer, come in conspicuous clusters.

Hedera ★★★
Ivy

Valuable plants, not just because of the huge variety of leaf shapes, sizes and colours but also because they grow almost anywhere, including dry shade. Most species are hardy and of these, some of the finest garden forms are descended either from *H. colchica*, whose leaves are large and oblong, or *H. helix* (English ivy).

Hydrangea petiolaris ★
Climbing hydrangea

Self-clinging plant which will grow in dense shade but flowers better in full light. Bright tan stems provide winter interest; fresh spring foliage; cream lacecap flowers arrive in early summer.

Jasminum ★
Jasmine

Both winter- and summer-flowering species can be combined with other climbers. Some are not fully frost hardy but *J. nudiflorum* is tough enough to flower during cold weather.

Lonicera ★★★
Honeysuckle

Essential climbers because of the speed with which many of them can cover unsightly objects. Most climbing species have beautiful flowers and the great majority are sweetly scented. *L. japonica* 'Halliana' is evergreen and flowers throughout summer and autumn; *L. periclymenum* has scented varieties for most of the growing season from 'Belgica' in spring, to 'Serotina' for mid-summer; *L. × tellmanniana* has startling orange blooms flecked with scarlet and in the red range, *L. × brownii* 'Dropmore Scarlet' is worthy.

Parthenocissus and relatives ★★
Virginia creeper

Vigorous, self-clinging climbers with good, fresh foliage which colours strongly in autumn. *P. quinquefolia* can cover an entire building with its five-lobed leaves which turn red in autumn but is a less tenacious self-clinger than *P. tricuspidata* (Boston ivy). *P. henryana* is less vigorous and inclined to suffer frost damage but has lovely purple foliage with silver markings.

Passiflora ★★★
Passion flower

Tender but vigorous enough to cover large areas in a short time. The hardiest is *P. caerulea*.

Rhodochiton atrosanguineus ★★★

Tender but easily grown from seed or cuttings which have been overwintered indoors. The twining stems are festooned with showy pink calyces housing dark maroon flowers.

Rosa (climbing and rambling) ★★
Rose

Along with clematis, roses are perhaps the most important plants for vertical gardening. They make good vehicles for herbaceous climbers and, in many gardens, provide more colour and interest than everything else. With rambling roses, the pruning mode is usually to remove all wood that has flowered and then to tie in new leads which will flower the following season. Climbing roses are, usually, less vigorous than ramblers. They can be pruned lightly, if a large framework is wanted or, on smaller buildings, pruned quite hard. Best for scent are 'Zéphirine Drouhin', wine pink; 'Lady Hillingdon', apricot; 'Madame Grégoire Staechelin', shell pink, good hips; 'Madame Isaac Pereire', deep pink. Good for red shades are: 'Guinée', darkest of all; 'Zigeunerknabe', scarlet; 'Dublin Bay'; 'Parkdirektor Riggers'. Pink shades include 'Albertine', salmon; 'New Dawn', pale pink; 'Bantry Bay', light rose pink. Yellow, apricot shades are 'Golden Showers'; 'Mermaid', single, yellow; 'Gloire de Dijon', buff; 'Maigold', salmon orange. White and cream shades: 'Albéric Barbier', lemon to white; 'Mme Alfred Carrière', white, pinkish in the bud; 'Wedding Day', vigorous rambler, small white flowers.

Solanum ★★★
Potato vine

S. jasminoides is tender and needs to grow on a warm wall but is worth seeking for its slate blue-grey flowers and yellow stamens. *S. crispum* is tougher, grows vigorously and has a constant succession of blue-and-yellow flowers.

Vitis ★★
Vine

The purple-leaved *V. vinifera* 'Purpurea' (grape vine) has dramatic foliage which intensifies in colour as it ages. *V. coignetiae* has huge, bronze-tinted leaves which turn to brilliant orange and red before falling in autumn.

KEY

▲ Acid or neutral soil only – lime haters

♠ Architectural quality – outstanding shapes

🖉 Deciduous – loses leaves in winter

♣ Evergreen

✿ Flowers (or fruits) – prized for blooming quality

🍃 Foliage – prized for leaves

▨ Drought tolerant

≋ Moisture-loving plants – not necessarily aquatics

● Shade-loving plants

☀ Sun-loving plants

❋ Tender in cold areas – barely frost hardy

✼ Plants which have some winter interest

Passiflora

Short-cut ratings are given for most plants.

★★★ Extra fast – bears results within a season

★★ Moderately fast – some results in the second season

★ Not especially fast – but still a good short-cut plant

PLANTS ESPECIALLY GOOD FOR CONTAINERS

Many of the plants mentioned so far will grow happily in containers but since container gardening is so much a part of the short-cut garden, here are some plants specifically for container use.

Abutilon ★★

Rapid, shrubby plants with generous foliage, often well marked, and colourful flowers whose petals surround a central spike of stamens. Good foliage forms include *A. pictum* 'Thompsonii' and *A. megapotamicum* 'Variegatum'. Colour forms of merit are *A.* 'Canary Bird' and *A.* 'Ashford Red'.

Agapanthus ★

Bulbous plants with strap-like leaves and flower spikes up to 1m/3ft topped with umbels of blue flowers. Most forms are tender and will not survive winter unless the compost in the container is protected from freezing. For cold areas, varieties bred from *A. campanulatus* are more likely to survive than those from *A. africanus*.

Argyranthemum frutescens ★★★

Formerly called *Chrysanthemum frutescens*. Rapid growth and a long flowering season with daisy-like flowers and mildly aromatic, cut leaves. There are various colours including pink, white and yellow. Easily rooted from cuttings.

Buxus sempervirens
Box

Not short-cut plants but useful in containers because they grow slowly and yet can be clipped into almost any shape.

Cistus ★★
Rock rose

Drought-resistant, reasonably hardy and often attractive in foliage as well as in flower, these shrubs are useful. Each flower lasts but a day. Large-flowered species include *C. × lusitanicus*, whose white petals have purple blotches at their bases, and *C. ladanifer*, also white, whose glutinous foliage is redolent of musk.

Diascia ★★★

Trailing plants, usually with pink flowers produced over long periods. One of the largest is *D. rigescens* whose stems stay more or less erect. *D. cordata* is a smaller plant but with lovely flowers.

Fuchsia ★★★

The mainstay of most summer planting. Many hundreds of varieties have been bred with new ones every year. Technically, they are shrubs but most are grown outdoors as temporary plants, to be lifted and overwintered indoors. They can be trained to cascade, grown into standards or cut back every year and grown as herbaceous plants.

Helichrysum petiolare ★★★

Silver foliage and trailing, wiry stems, make this the perfect 'back-up' plant for almost all mixed container plantings but it is fine on its own.

Impatiens ★★★
Busy Lizzie

Flower profusely for most of the growing season and flower well in shade. The stems are rather brittle, the leaves glossy and the flattened flowers clean in colours. Hues range from white through orange, pearl pink, red and magenta.

Laurus nobilis ★

Not a short-cut plant but, like box, useful because of its suitability for clipping in a formal container. The leaves are aromatic and, when they arrive, the little primrose yellow flowers are quite pleasant too.

Lobelia erinus ★★★

Besides the ubiquitous blues, there are now white and mixed shades of pinkish purple.

Pelargonium ★★★
Pot geranium

The bewildering number of colours, sizes and habits increases every year. Many of the species have aromatic foliage. Most of the upright varieties have been bred either from *P. zonale* (pot geranium), or *P. regale* (regal pelargonium). Trailing varieties are from *P. peltatum* (ivy leaf pelargonium). Many of the variegated forms are old varieties which can only be reproduced from cuttings.

Petunia ★★★

These drought-resistant plants come in practically every colour under the sun except for true yellow or orange. Most of the seed offered is of F1 hybrids, bred for exceptional vigour and for especially clean colour and large flowers. There are stripes, ruffles, doubles, singles and so on.

Diascia

Tropaeolum ★★★

Most trailing species of this genus are better suited to the open garden but the two exceptions are *T. peregrinum* (canary creeper), whose flowers are deeply lobed and bright yellow, and *T. majus* (nasturtium). Some nasturtium strains are better behaved than others and, for containers, it is safer to go for a compact variety unless you do not object to garlands of bright orange and yellow flowers by the yard. *T.* 'Alaska' has white variegations on the foliage.

Verbena ★★

Especially good for hanging baskets or trailing over the sides of window boxes. There are a number of good species to choose from, including *V. peruviania*. Collectable varieties include *V.* 'White Cascade', *V.* 'Sissinghurst', pink, and *V.* 'Silver Anne', all of which are easy to propagate by cuttings.

Viola ★★★

Pansy, heartsease

Winter-flowering pansies, which bloom throughout autumn, winter and spring, are one of the mainstays of winter planting schemes for containers. They are easy to grow from seed, in self-coloured groups or in mixtures, and come in a range of clean colours which include the usual pansy bicolors as well as plain blue, apricot, tan or yellow. There are plenty of other violas, from boisterous giant-flowered pansies to tiny, delicate violets.

WATER PLANTS

Most water plants are excellent for the short-cut garden because they are such rapid developers. However, certain species are even quicker, providing that sought-after maturity within a single season. Do remember that what is a rapid developer in year one may well become an invasive nuisance thereafter. You have been warned!

Most of these plants will grow in or out of water.

Butomus umbellatus

Flowering rush

Lovely pink umbels of flowers held well above the water on stiff stems.

Caltha palustris

Kingcup, marsh marigold

Huge yellow blooms in spring above rounded foliage. Seeds freely.

Cardamine pratensis 'Flore Pleno'

Cuckoo flower

Double form, with lilac flowers in spring on 30cm/1ft stems. Clump forming.

Iris pseudacorus

Yellow flag

Lovely in all its garden varieties, especially the form with variegated foliage. 2m/6ft.

Lythrum salicaria

Purple loosestrife

Willowy foliage and purple spires of bloom in midsummer.

Mimulus guttatus

Monkey flower

Successional yellow blooms with red spots in their throats throughout summer and into early autumn. A rapid seeder.

Myosotis scorpioides

Water forget-me-not

The largest flowers of all the forget-me-nots and a glorious sky blue. Flowers throughout summer.

Nymphaea

Water lily

Produces floating foliage within a week or two of planting. Brightly coloured flowers in summer. It is important to match the lily to the size and depth of your pond. Buying one that is too vigorous in the hopes that it will develop more quickly will prove to have been a false economy. Fading leaves needs to be removed to prevent them polluting the water.

Osmunda regalis

Royal fern

This stately fern is equally happy in or out of the water as long as it is in acid or neutral conditions. The large fronds grow to 2m/6ft and there are separate fruiting branches.

Ranunculus lingua

Great spearwort

Huge buttercup flowers on 1m/3ft stems. Very invasive.

Sagittaria sagittifolia

Common arrowhead

Arrow-shaped leaves. The three-petalled, white flowers are held well above the water. Invasive.

Zantedeschia aethiopica

Arum lily

The flowers are, in fact, white spathes. In cold climates these are best grown under water to prevent the roots from becoming frozen.

KEY

- ◤ Acid or neutral soil only – lime haters
- ♠ Architectural quality – outstanding shapes
- Ø Deciduous – loses leaves in winter
- ♣ Evergreen
- ✿ Flowers (or fruits) – prized for blooming quality
- ✔ Foliage – prized for leaves
- ✸ Drought tolerant
- ≋ Moisture-loving plants – not necessarily aquatics
- ● Shade-loving plants
- ☀ Sun-loving plants
- ✳ Tender in cold areas – barely frost hardy
- ✄ Plants which have some winter interest

Tropaeolum

10

SHORT CUTS TO GARDEN MAINTENANCE

It is a great pity that so many people allow themselves to be put off gardening because they think it might involve them in too much hard work. Garden writers, designers and sundry experts, have contributed to this false thinking by expending far too much time and thought on trying, in vain, to develop maintenance-free gardens. There are, of course, no such things, any more than there is a perpetual motion machine or a self-cooking breakfast, but, rather than lamenting that fact, we should rejoice in it!

The misconception lies in that dreaded word 'maintenance'. If to you it represents backbreaking labour or a series of boring chores, you have got it wrong. Maintaining a garden – a well-planted, thoughtfully designed one – can be a rich source of pleasure. It gets you amongst the plants where you can enjoy their distinctive characteristics close at hand.

Brick paving keeps maintenance work to a minimum in this part of a garden. Borders should be checked regularly for emerging weeds.

PRACTICAL DESIGN
Plan with maintenance in mind

OPTIMIZE POTENTIAL
Provide an ideal environment

ROUTINE MAINTENANCE
Keep chores small scale

ABOVE *A packed summer border in full flower leaves little room for weeds to grow. Vigilance, however, will help to prevent any weeds from seeding among mature plants.*

There was a time when duties in the garden were the responsibility of the head gardener. If you could afford a house with a garden, you could afford a gardener. Hard labour was the main input – it was the gardener's job – and joy in the beauty of it all was the owner's by right. Nowadays, when you have to be rich to employ a part-time gardener and very rich to have a head gardener, the physical input is up to you as well as the joyful outcome. But since we garden for joy and not for a wage, it is important that the input has as strong an element of satisfaction as the result. Make that maxim part of your garden philosophy, and maintenance will become a pleasure, not a burden.

The way to enjoy garden maintenance is to make sure that it never gets on top of you. In that respect, it is rather like servicing a debt by instalments: if you skip a payment, the problem magnifies alarmingly quickly. With gardens, routine maintenance is usually pretty straightforward and need not be time consuming. But, left undone for a while, the small chore becomes a large task and soon escalates to a serious problem. The moral: keep on top.

Design plays an important part in the level of maintenance needed. For example, being a fanatical plant collector, I have far too many borders, all of which require a lot of weeding.

That suits me at present but, as I age and decrepitude reduces my waning vigour, no doubt I will have to pave over several borders or re-plant them with thicker populations of ground cover to reduce the work. Similarly, alpine enthusiasts are more prepared than the average gardener to undertake the laborious task of weeding their rock gardens. Those who love to feed, roll and generally nurture their lawns will probably have a lot of grass in their gardens. Others may prefer stone flags. It is a matter of preference.

As far as short-cut gardening is concerned, maintenance is important but the priorities may be different. Since speed is the essence, it follows that the aim must be to optimize the plants' development. You can do this by providing the ideal environment and then ensuring that the odds are continually shortened in the plants' favour.

The whole concept of maintenance is locked up in three key areas: soil conditioning and feeding; weeding and pest control; and propagation. Get these three right, add a little pruning, training and plant care and you have the whole garden under control. The following pages outline the principles of short-cut garden maintenance to ensure maximum speed and performance in return for minimum input.

SOIL CONDITIONING AND FEEDING

Before looking at the condition of your plants, it is important to know what your soil is like. Although good soil is not essential to good gardening – many of the world's finest gardens are on indifferent land – care of the soil is crucial. It is important to maintain a good, workable soil structure – one which roots can penetrate with ease.

Soil in good heart holds moisture yet drains freely. This may appear to be a contradiction but even the lightest sandy soils, if they contain good levels of organic material, will stay reasonably moist even though heavy rain percolates through them with the greatest of ease. This is because the organic particles absorb and hold water, while the surplus runs straight through.

It seems a paradox that incorporating fibrous organic material will have a lightening or leavening effect on heavy soil as well as adding body to a sandy loam, but it is true. Organic detritus improves permeability and enhances absorbability.

Heavy soils need more care than light sands. Although potentially more fertile, they are easier to put out of condition. Even if drainage is good, heavy soils can be spoilt by compaction. Just walking on them while they are wet will press the particles together, driving out the air and thus making the soil impenetrable for roots.

The three golden rules for improving soil condition, therefore, are to ensure that drainage is adequate, to keep building up its organic content, and avoid compacting heavy soil by keeping yourself and heavy equipment off it as much as possible.

There are no short cuts to good soil condition but, fortunately, developing the quality of soil is not especially long winded. It is important to keep up the treatment for as long as you garden, and the overall condition will show a steady improvement over decades, but the first attempt will also produce fruitful results.

▶ **Speed up the time it takes compost to convert from dead flower stalks and twigs to the bulky, crumbly material so useful as a soil improver by investing in a mechanical compost shredder. Blend potentially soggy material, such as lawn mowings, with drier, more woody fragments to further improve the texture of the compost.**

▶ **In poor soil make local sites to get your key plants off to a good start. Dig holes larger than the new trees and shrubs need and mix in either special tree-planting compost or a blend of rotted manure, friable garden compost and some slow-release fertilizer. As these first plants develop, they will help to create their own microclimate and hence improve the environment.**

▶ **Repair any damage. If soil has been spoilt, perhaps, by builders or unskilled gardening predecessors, you must try to put things right before you plant. Deep digging helps, especially if you can leave the ground rough and let the frost work on it. Failing that, try to break up compacted soil as best you can with a garden fork or spade, incorporating bulky material at the same time. Do not attempt this, however, unless the ground is reasonably dry or you could do more harm than good by compacting damp soil.**

BELOW *Just about any soil can be improved by additions of compost and fertilizer to make it capable of producing fine crops of vegetables, fruit or flowers, but it will need to be maintained in good condition.*

GOOD DRAINAGE
Improve soil condition

PROTECT SOIL
Avoid compaction

CONDITION SOIL
Replenish organic content
regularly

CONSERVE WATER
Cover soil with a mulch

▶ **If you find your soil is in poor condition, it will pay to incorporate a lot more in the way of compost or rotted manure than you would in a normal routine year. You will enjoy the results of having done this as soon as the new plants are in!**

PLANT NOURISHMENT

There is often confusion about which materials feed plants and which enhance the soil. Plants manufacture most of their tissue from a combination of atmospheric carbon dioxide and water obtained from the soil. The material they get out of the ground consists only of essential elements. These are nitrogen, phosphorus and potassium, in relatively large quantities, and minerals such as iron, copper and cobalt in much smaller quantities. The big three nutrients, often referred to as NPK, are usually the first to run short and most gardeners add them fairly regularly, either from a fertilizer bag – there are hundreds of proprietary brands – or in the form of animal manure.

Garden compost, peat or leaf mould alone will not provide these essential nutrients. Their

ABOVE *Bark mulch improves the soil's ability to retain moisture. It also conditions the soil, which will benefit this humus-loving* Arisaema candidissimum.

function is, rather, to improve the physical structure of the soil and, in fact, they may increase the need for nitrogen since the micro-organisms in them compete with the plants for it. So, adding plant nutrients is a completely different exercise from conditioning the soil, but both jobs are important.

▶ **Plant food, especially in the form of rotted manure, may take a while to work. To speed up their growth rate, try giving your plants a foliar feed. The easiest way to do this is to spray the foliage with a proprietary brand of liquid fertilizer in a dilute form. New plants, especially bedding, benefit from a 'pop up' solution of liquid fertilizer, applied as they are watered in immediately after planting.**

The function of a mulch is to help soil retain moisture. It consists of a layer of bulky material such as bark chippings, dry, rotted compost or leaf mould, spread over the soil's surface to reduce evaporation. Some mulches have the added advantage of suppressing weeds.

Unless they are made from animal wastes or contain added nutrients, mulches do not provide the essential nutrients.

THE ROUTINE

Soil conditioning is an ongoing task but, fortunately, one that needs doing only once a year, usually in winter or early spring. In a new garden, after the initial incorporation of organic matter, subsequent applications can be simply as an annual mulch spread on the surface. If you miss a year no great harm will ensue, as long as your land is in good heart. Your plants will tell you when conditions have become less than ideal for them.

When to feed depends on the plants. Once they are established, few trees or shrubs need feeding at all, unless, like roses, you are regularly pruning off a great deal. Perennials are content with a single annual dressing of fertilizer – I use a granular compound at the manufacturer's recommended rate – but annuals, especially if they grow in containers, need feeding more frequently. Bedded annuals in my garden get two or three applications of compound fertilizer per season, but container plants have a weekly liquid feed throughout summer to keep them in good health.

WEEDING AND PEST CONTROL

One year's seed, they say, is ten years' weed. And that sums up the whole approach to weed control. It is a matter of discipline. By preventing weeds from seeding or spreading, the task of weed control is made simple. Once you have allowed an infestation to proliferate, what might have been a spot treatment becomes a major operation.

In a new garden, it is essential to start clean. But it is much easier to sort out a weed problem on a bare site, with a blanket approach, than to try to eliminate weeds from an established, or worse, a half-established border. Even if cleaning up the weeds delays your planting by as much as a season, it may be quicker – and more trouble free in subsequent years – to put your planting dates back until you know that your ground is clean.

PROBLEM PERENNIALS

Perennial weeds are the ones that will destroy your peace of mind. Creeping grasses, buttercup, bindweed, stinging nettle and docks are all pernicious and often seem indestructible. Each can proliferate from a tiny root fragment.

▶ On a bare site, spray the growing weeds with glyphosate. When they have died, work the land, allow it to green over and hit it again with a second spray.

▶ Alternatively, if the area is small enough – or if you are an organic gardener – dig out all the roots and then peg a layer of thick black polythene over the soil surface and leave it there for a couple of months at least. When you lift it, all the roots underneath may be dead. But do not bank on it!

▶ In an established but weedy garden, all you can do is select areas for spot treatment. If you work over the land a bit at a time eventually you will gain control.

▶ Where there are really bad infestations, it may be worth your while sacrificing a whole area just to get it cleaned up. Do not assume that if the perennial weeds do not reappear immediately, they have been killed. Roots could lie dormant and produce new plants, months or even a year later.

CONTROLLING ANNUALS

Annual weeds are easier to deal with than perennials. The only way they can reproduce is by seed, so, if you prevent them from seeding you will eliminate them. With the larger ones, it is just a question of being vigilant. Spot a sow thistle or an annual nettle before it flowers and you have avoided a potential problem. Miss it because it lurked behind a shrub and within a season you have an infestation.

Small annuals can be more troublesome. The loathsome hairy bittercress (*Cardamine hirsuta*) has been haunting garden centres since they began. It seldom grows more than a few centimetres high but catapults its seeds in all directions – often into your eye when you are trying to pull it out – and is capable of greening over a whole border in a few weeks. Cleanliness, that is, preventing weeds from gaining a toehold, is essential if you want your borders to develop colonies of self-perpetuating garden plants at optimum speed.

▶ Use a hoe to work soil between plants before annual weed seedlings have a chance to flower; take care that you do not damage seedlings of garden plants.

▶ A thick mulch can be effective for keeping down annual weeds, but has the disadvantage of limiting the extent to which your plants can seed themselves.

WEED RECOGNITION

When you survey your borders in spring, and you see that the soil is beginning to burgeon with tiny green seedlings, what do you do? Hoe them out and you may be sacrificing some lovely garden plants along with the enemy. An alternative action is to weed selectively.

It is surprisingly easy to learn to recognize weed seedlings, even when they are only showing their first leaves. There are reference books on the subject – agricultural students have weed seedling recognition tests *ad nauseam* – and, once you have observed the illustrations, the real thing will be easy enough to identify. Obviously, if the infestation is bad, it may be necessary to sling the baby out with the bath water but, so often, it is possible to select and destroy the weeds and thus make more room for the desired seedlings to thrive.

ERADICATE PERENNIALS
Root out and spray

PREVENT ANNUALS SEEDING
Hoe little, but often

RECOGNIZE WEEDS
Distinguish between weeds and plants

ABOVE *Unless roses are disease-resistant strains, they should be treated regularly against fungus and black spot to keep them healthy and in bloom.*

PESTS AND DISEASES

To develop at top speed, plants need to be in rude health as well as happy in their environment. Anything that slows development is working against the short-cut garden and, since pests and diseases can arrest plant development, they must be seen as being anti short cut. However, with so much concern these days about the environment, one wonders whether there is any place in our private, ornamental gardens for pesticides at all.

I have to confess that I do use fungicides, albeit in very limited quantities, on my roses and certain other plants. It simply is not possible to prevent mildew and black spot from affecting roses without chemical control. Nevertheless, I am convinced that we can minimize pest and disease problems by management rather than with chemicals.

▶ If you are not organic, a prophylactic fungicide programme on susceptible plants, such as roses or *Aster novi-belgii* cultivars, will ensure sustained, healthy growth.

▶ Many modern plants have been bred for vigour and resistance to specific diseases and these are always worth selecting, provided they are good garden plants in every other respect. Growing *Aster novae-angliae*, which does not get mildew, instead of *Aster novi-belgii*, which does, is a pretty obvious solution.

▶ Whenever there is a choice of several different roses with similar colours and characters, clearly, the more disease resistant are the ones to select. Among shrub roses, the rugosas are especially resistant to mildew and I have yet to see one with black spot.

But I love the huge single rose 'Complicata' which gets terrible black spot and the climber 'Zéphirine Drouhin' which is a regular martyr to mildew. These two roses cannot be substituted. They have been in cultivation for more than a century and are unique. What is the solution?

▶ Select the site with care: avoid planting mildew-prone roses in warm, dry positions. Make sure they are so well fed and healthy that the effects of disease are minimized. Damaging insects such as aphids, mealy bug, vine weevil and red spider mite should also be kept under control by whatever means you consider ethically acceptable. Without control, any of these pests could delay growth and cancel out a short cut.

PLANT PROPAGATION

Once your soil is in good condition, with fertility maximized and weeds minimized, the other aspect of maintenance concerns the plants themselves. This is by far the most enjoyable part because the results of your labours are so tangible.

You do not need to be a gifted horticulturist to be able to multiply your own plants. Plant experts sometimes like to play on the mystery of propagation, probably to make it look difficult and therefore to make them look clever. Certain plants are, without doubt, troublesome and fussy about their requirements but, of the tens of thousands in cultivation today, the great majority are simple to increase in number.

The short-cut garden will be hungry for new plants, especially in its first months. You can purchase all your requirements but it may be more sensible, especially if the garden is being developed on a tight budget, to produce at least a proportion of these at home. Basic propagating skills – growing from seed, taking cuttings and plant division – are therefore essential for successful short-cut gardening. Division is the simplest but growing from seed is the most exciting.

SOWING SEED

It is hardly relevant, in a book on short-cut gardening, to wax lyrical about growing such slow developers as trees or bulbs from seed. These take years to reach maturity and, absorbing though the exercise is, you need not to be in a hurry for results! But all annuals and biennials, many perennials and certain woody plants are quick and easy to start from seed.

▶ **You can grow tender subjects such as petunias or lobelias reasonably easily if you provide bottom heat and plenty of light as they develop. A greenhouse is ideal for this, preferably equipped with an electric propagator which maintains the compost at a steady temperature of around 20°C/68°F and makes an ideal environment for such seeds to germinate.**

▶ **You can grow seedlings on a windowsill, using a windowsill propagator, if you have not got a greenhouse but, as daylight is likely to be in short supply in such a location, the seedlings will tend to be weaker and more leggy.**

Hygiene with seed raising is crucial. A sterile, ready-made compost is probably best, watered with clean tapwater at least until the seedlings have been pricked out and are growing away vigorously. Using rainwater and sowing in unsterilized compost will lead to failure.

▶ **To sow seed, first fill a seed tray or a pot with sterile seed compost, level off the surface and firm it gently. Soak the compost carefully, either by standing the tray in water or by sprinkling with a watering can and rose until the water runs through to the bottom, then allow it to drain off for a while. Scatter seeds sparingly onto the surface, covering the seeds only if advised on the packet – some species need light to germinate, others require darkness. Finally, place the tray or pot in the propagator until the seeds germinate and the seedlings are green and healthy.**

▶ **Prick out seedlings into compost-filled pots or larger trays as soon as the seedlings are large enough to handle. By now they will be growing very fast but do not place them outdoors until the danger of frost has passed. Harden off the young plants in a cold frame before planting them out in their final positions.**

PROLIFERATE PLANTS
Sow seeds and take cuttings

FAST SEEDS
Choose quick developers

TENDER PLANTS
Sow in a propagator

AIM FOR SUCCESS
Follow instructions

CONTROL OVERCROWDING
Be ruthless with overgrown interim plants

ABOVE *Correct care and regular watering of young seedlings is essential for them to thrive. Diligence in the early stages of a plant's life will result in strong, healthy plants.*

▶ A useful short-cut alternative to sowing seeds yourself is to buy ready germinated seedlings. Various firms sell these and they offer a quick solution if your time and your propagating space are limited.

Hardy herbaceous plants are much easier to start than tender ones. Few need bottom heat and none of them needs any protection. A cold frame is useful, if only because it enables you to keep the seed pans in one place, but any quiet corner of the garden will do as a germination zone. Most perennials can be sown in the same way as described above for half hardies. The compost can be a little grittier and it is a good idea to put a thin layer of sharp grit on the surface of the tray or pan to discourage the growth of moss or algae. I place my perennial seed pans in a lidless frame, sheltered from direct sunlight by a low wall. The aim is to ensure as constant a temperature as possible and to prevent the pans from drying out or baking in the sun.

Seeds germinate in response to different stimuli so, whereas some will pop up in days, others may take months. Many species, especially hardy primulas, meconopsis and clematis, need to be stratified by frost action before they will sprout. I leave the weather to do this naturally over the winter months but there are short cuts.

BELOW *Self-seeding foxgloves have quickly established a block of tall colour at the edge of a belt of young trees.*

▶ To hasten the germination of seeds that need stratification, mix the seed with about five times its volume of fine, damp sand, place in a waterproof envelope and refrigerate, or even deep freeze, for about ten days. Immediately after this, sow the sand-and-seed mixture in the usual way.

In a short-cut garden, where self seeding is encouraged, much of the propagation takes care of itself. Self-perpetuating colonies of plants will develop without aid but often the seedlings end up in the wrong place. The best plants usually end up in the lawn or at the back of the border but it is never difficult to move them to where they will look better.

Other plants that have seeded for me with far more success than I have achieved myself include paeonies, *Daphne tangutica*, *Clematis viticella* and herbaceous penstemons. As for aquilegias, I have a nice collection of a dozen sorts but have not sown a seed for decades. All I do is keep the different varieties in different parts of the garden and weed out any inferior or impure stock once it has flowered.

▶ It is easy enough to lift as many errant seedlings as you want and relocate them. While you are about it, prepare the ground with a little extra soil conditioner and fertilizer to give the plants a boost and then leave the rest to nature.

CUTTINGS

Most perennial plants will grow from cuttings as will almost all trees and shrubs. This is, without doubt, the cheapest and quickest way of propagating plants, particularly if the original cuttings are scrounged from friends or neighbours! All you need to do is take a young, growing sprig of the plant – preferably one without any flowers or flower buds on it – trim off the lower leaves, cut across the stem cleanly, and insert it into compost.

▶ To take successful cuttings, select young material for cutting – shoots from immature plants root easily – choosing only clean, disease-free material. Place the cuttings in sterile compost, preferably one which contains sharp grit to stimulate rooting. As soon as they have rooted, pot the cuttings up.

You can also strike cuttings of woody plants. This method is especially useful for vigorous shrubs which throw up wands of growth each year. Privet, for example, will root readily this way, as will shrub roses and willows. Box, too, will quietly root itself over the period of a year. This means that if you have a large stock of such species, you will be able to root your own hedges.

▶ To take cuttings of woody plants, select young but ripening stems in the autumn, and stick these into sheltered ground which has been worked to improve it. If you are able to arrange for a constant temperature and some protection from their drying out too much, your success rate will be quite high.

▶ The quickest cuttings of all are those taken with a tiny piece of root attached. Perennial violas, for example, are traditionally raised from cuttings but, if you cut a little lower down the stem, you end up with a single shoot and a couple of roots. These flower weeks earlier than normal cuttings, and are especially useful if you lack a greenhouse for propagating.

SPECIAL PROBLEMS

One aspect of maintenance that is more irksome in the short-cut garden than anywhere else is the problem of overgrowing. When you are in a hurry and have planted rampant species, you must expect an element of overcrowding. Within a couple of seasons, there will be a number of large plants to dig out and destroy.

This will sorely test your resolve. Which ones should you remove? How can you bring yourself to kill a healthy shrub? But unless you are ruthless, you will rue the day! The big, pushy shrubs will probably become leggy within another few seasons, will overshadow their neighbours and become nuisances. Each season, therefore, remind yourself of your medium-term plans. Plants you introduced merely for that first rush of growth, but never intended to keep, should be removed – unless circumstances have changed and they are now needed.

When they first go, these monsters may leave scars in the form of misshapen neighbours or holes in the planting. But you will be surprised at how quickly these will heal, especially if you tidy up the remaining plants, cutting off any drawn and straggly growth, and applying a little therapeutic fertilizer to the soil.

ABOVE *Whether destined for the vegetable garden or ornamental borders, young plants need to be hardened off in cold frames before being planted out. Cold frames can also be used for sowing hardy seeds.*

INDEX

ACKNOWLEDGMENTS

The publisher thanks the following photographers and organizations for their kind permission to reproduce the photographs in this book:

1 Michael Boys/Boys Syndication; 2–3 IPC Magazines 1992/Robert Harding Picture Library; 4–5 Clive Nichols (Coates Manor, West Sussex); 6 Brian Carter/Garden Picture Library; 7 Ron Sutherland/Garden Picture Library; 8–9 Andrew Lawson; 10 Marianne Majerus; 11–13 Brigitte Thomas; 14–5 Clay Perry/Garden Picture Library; 16 S & O Mathews; 17 John Glover/Garden Picture Library; 18 Gary Rogers/Garden Picture Library; 20 Jacqui Hurst/Boys Syndication; 22 Elizabeth Whiting and Associates; 23 Michael Boys/Boys Syndication; 24 Ron Sutherland/Garden Picture Library; 26 Rodney Hyett/Elizabeth Whiting and Associates; 28 Tim Sandall; 29 Tania Midgley; 30 Lynne Brotchie/Garden Picture Library; 31 Henk Dijkman/Garden Picture Library; 32 Steven Wooster/Garden Picture Library; 34 Clay Perry/Garden Picture Library; 36–7 Christopher Simon Sykes/Camera Press; 38–40 Brigitte Thomas; 41 Ron Sutherland/Garden Picture Library; 45 Neil Holmes; 46 Clive Nichols (Designer: Myles Challis); 47–9 Brigitte Thomas; 50–1 Clive Nichols (Designer: Anthony Noel); 52 Marianne Majerus; 53 above Brigitte Thomas; 53 below Tim Sandall; 54 Andreas von Einsiedel/Elizabeth Whiting and Associates; 55 Juliette Wade; 57 left Jerry Harpur/Elizabeth Whiting and Associates; 57 right Brigitte Thomas; 58 Peter Woloszynski/Elizabeth Whiting and Associates; 59 Ann Kelley/Garden Picture Library; 60 Clive Nichols (Coates Manor, West Sussex); 63 above Brigitte Thomas; 63 below Jacqui Hurst/Boys Syndication; 64–5 Michael Boys/Boys Syndication; 66 Stephen Robson/Garden Picture Library; 67 Jerry Pavia/Garden Picture Library; 68 Michèle Lamotagne/Garden Picture Library; 69 Henk Dijkman/Garden Picture Library; 70–1 above Jerry Harpur ('Dolwen', Powys); 71 below Jerry Harpur/Elizabeth Whiting and Associates; 72 Clive Nichols (Preen Manor, Shropshire); 73 Michael Boys/Boys Syndication; 74 John Glover/Garden Picture Library; 75 Clive Nichols (University Botanic Garden, Cambridge); 76 Ron Sutherland/Garden Picture Library; 78 Clive Nichols (Yew Tree Cottage, West Sussex); 79 above John Glover; 79 below Clive Nichols (Bourton House, Gloucestershire); 80–1 Christopher Simon Sykes/Camera Press; 82 Clive Nichols (Preen Manor, Shropshire); 83 above John Glover/Garden Picture Library; 83 below Michael Nicholson/Elizabeth Whiting and Associates; 84 above John Baker/Garden Picture Library; 84 below John Glover/Garden Picture Library; 85–86 above Joanne Pavia/Garden Picture Library; 86 below Brigitte Thomas; 87 Clive Nichols (Designer: Anthony Noel); 89 Steven Wooster/Garden Picture Library; 90 above John Glover; 90 below W.A. Lord; 91 John Glover; 92 above Neil Lorimer/Elizabeth Whiting and Associates; 92 below Christopher Simon Sykes/Camera Press; 93 S & O Mathews; 94–5 John Glover; 96 Hugh Palmer; 97 above Ron Sutherland/Garden Picture Library; 97 below Nedra Westwater/Elizabeth Whiting and Associates; 98 John Glover; 99 above Clive Nichols (Brook Cottage, Oxfordshire); 99 below John Glover; 100 Jerry Harpur/Elizabeth Whiting and Associates; 101 Steven Wooster/Garden Picture Library; 102 W.A. Lord; 103 David Askham/Garden Picture Library; 104–5 Jerry Harpur ('Dolwen', Powys); 107 John Glover; 118–9 W.A. Lord; 120 Clive Nichols (Brook Cottage, Oxfordshire); 124 Tim Sandall; 126 Bob Estall/Garden Picture Library; 130–1 Michael Boys/Boys Syndication; 132 Neil Holmes; 133 Clive Nichols (Ivy Cottage, Dorset); 134 John Glover; 136 Georges Lévêque; 137 Debbie Patterson; 138 S & O Mathews; 139 Debbie Patterson.